THE BOOK OF THE

BATH

FRANÇOISE DE BONNEVILLE

RIZZOLI
NEW YORK

CONTENTS

First published in the United States of America in 1998 by
RIZZOLI INTERNATIONAL PUBLICATIONS, INC.
300 Park Avenue South, New York, NY 10010

Translated from the French *Le Livre du bain*
by Jane Brenton

Copyright © 1997 Flammarion, Paris
English translation copyright © 1998
Thames and Hudson Ltd, London
and Rizzoli International Publications, Inc.

ISBN 0-8478-2134-X
LC 98-65882

Printed in Italy

THE STORY OF WATER

THE BATH is the ultimate celebration of the modern cult of the body, a moment of pleasure that is pure self-indulgence, pure delight. The very idea conjures up irresistibly the intimate space of the bathroom, fragrant soaps, soft sponges, balmy oils and tangy eaux de Cologne. And water itself, so obvious that you almost forget it. Water in abundance. The invigorating running water of the shower streaming over your skin. The warm, maternal comfort of the bath that cocoons your whole body.

We have made our ablutions since time immemorial, but the bath or daily shower taken under our own roof is a recent invention, and for good reason, since water was not piped to private dwellings until the second half of the nineteenth century – and then only to the kitchen. We must await the beginning of the twentieth century for the advent of the modern bathroom. Of course, humankind had not languished all that time without discovering the pleasures of bathing. Nature was always there, offering the refreshment of its seas, rivers, lakes and even healing springs, some of which rose already hot and bubbling. Water was nature's gift, and gradually, in every civilization, it acquired a variety of symbolic meanings. More than ever, these lie at the heart of the practice of bathing today.

The story of the bath is written perforce with a pen dipped in the inkwell of the oceans, rivers and springs. It is the history of the 'primitive sensuality' of the body's relationship to water. And the history first and foremost of fresh running water, which, as the philosopher Gaston Bachelard writes in *L'eau et les rêves*, best satisfies 'the need we have to experience a thing directly, to touch it and to taste it – the principal reason for the perceived superiority of spring water to the water of the oceans'. It is spring water, 'the true water of myth, the water that refreshes and slakes one's thirst', that peoples of all times and all places have worshipped, deified and regarded as sacred. The Egyptians made a cult of the Nile. The Assyrians and the Chaldeans worshipped rivers in general, and the Phoenicians revered the sources of the river Adonis. The Greeks invented a goddess of springs, whom they called Artemis, and the Buddhist religion made the Ganges the sacred river of India.

Over the centuries, mankind has invested this magical, flowing water with various symbolic meanings revolving around myths of creation and rebirth.

IN THE Young Woman Preparing for Her Bath *(page 1), painted by Jules Scalbert at the end of the nineteenth century, the protagonist leans towards the swan's-neck tap with a movement that is – already – mechanical and abstracted, even though running water was a very recently introduced amenity. The mood is quite different in Pierre Bonnard's* The Bath *(pages 2–3), which conveys the sheer physical pleasure of stretching out at full length in the water. The bathtub may be the preferred form of bath in the West, but the hammam prevails in the East. In the detail of Gérôme's* The Moorish Bath *of 1874 (page 4), one can almost hear the lapping of the cool water and the splashes of ablutions at the marble fountains.* The Bath, *painted by Charles Gleyre in 1868 (above), shows a mother preparing to bathe her child with great gentleness. For us, the circular basin in the Graeco-Roman atrium depicted is inevitably reminiscent of the baptismal font of Christianity. Another biblical theme, nudity surprised or innocence abused, is represented by the story of Susannah, spied on by two elders while bathing. Admirable for its blend of delicacy and sensuality, this* Susannah at the Bath *(facing page) was painted by Jean-Baptiste Santerre in 1704, as part of a decorative scheme featuring the thermal baths of antiquity.*

PURIFYING WATER

'In water, the material imagination finds pure matter par excellence, matter that is naturally pure. It is a constant temptation therefore to endow it with the facile symbolism of purity,' argues Gaston Bachelard. Almost from the first moment when men invented gods and the rites in which to worship them, the notion of purification became attached to acts of ritual ablution. To purify oneself in clear water before rendering homage to the gods has been part of the ceremonial of every religion since earliest antiquity.

In Egypt, people bathed their face and hands in water before offering up their prayers to Isis, while priests washed their bodies at least twice each night and twice each day.

In the Old Testament, there are numerous texts celebrating water. In Psalm 51, the prophet praises it as a symbol of purity: '...in secret you teach me wisdom. Purify me with hyssop till I am clean, wash me till I am whiter than snow.'

Yet water did not properly become a symbol of the spiritual life until the New Testament era, when Christianity was quick to readopt the lustral bath prescribed by Moses, in which matter and spirit coincided for the first time. John baptized the first Christians in the river Jordan, an act that was not replaced until much later (around the seventh century AD) by the simple expedient of sprinkling water on the forehead. According to Tertullian, the famous Christian apologist of the second century, water possessed innate qualities of purification. Being holy, it could remove all taint and open the way to a new state of being. All the prophets of the great religions – Manu, Buddha, Confucius, Moses and Mohammed – made capital of these 'moral' attributes of water, prescribing ablutions as part of their teachings, until eventually water came to be seen as 'cleansing the soul' as well as the body.

In India, according to the Rigveda (the anthology of Vedic holy scriptures) water has the power to give life, strength and purity in the spiritual as well as the physical realm. Brahmans bathe once or twice a day in rivers or holy pools; they rinse their face, hands and mouth several times a day and are obliged to purify themselves immediately whenever they are contaminated by dirt.

In Japan, Buddhist rituals dating back to the sixth century AD proved entirely consistent with Shinto-ism, in which bodily health and spiritual purity are

THE SAME theme but an entirely different atmosphere is depicted in this Susannah and the Elders *(above), its cultivated high style characteristic of the Mannerist Renaissance; it is a masterpiece of the famous Venetian painter Tintoretto, who worked almost exclusively on religious themes.* Bathsheba's Bath *(facing page) shows another biblical character who was favourite subject among painters. The story is that David fell hopelessly in love with Bathsheba, wife of Uriah, when he surprised her in all her naked beauty in the bath. So that he could marry her himself, he sent her husband away to die in battle. This painting by Sebastiano Ricci (1659–1734), one of the forerunners of European Rococo painting, shows Bathsheba at the moment when, unconsciously aware that David's gaze is upon her, she lowers her eyes. The presence of the Moorish servant gives a clue as to the period, while the water, timeless heart of the ritual, is indicated by the presence of an elaborate metal ewer.*

inextricably linked. Like most other religions, Shintoism equates immorality with dirtiness and virtue with cleanliness. The Shinto bath is part of a whole sequence of purification exercises, and, even today, places of pilgrimage echo to the sound of the ancient rites. Before entering the precinct of the baths themselves, a person's first act must be to take water and rinse the mouth and hands.

In the Jewish religion, the ritual bath or *mikveh* is important, once again, for its purifying qualities. Bathing is prescribed by the law of Moses, and the Talmud specifies that no Jew may live in a town without public baths. The *mikveh* is not a cleansing bath, since one must wash oneself before entering it. It is reserved for women and involves the total immersion of the body in pure water at specific and significant moments in a woman's lifetime: before marriage (the only bath for which there exists a male equivalent), after a couple have been separated for a period of twelve days (signifying the recommencement of sexual activity), after childbirth, after a journey or after touching a dead body.

The construction of the *mikveh* was laid down precisely. The water had to be not standing but natural running water. A hole was therefore dug in order to locate a spring, a subterranean river or ground water (*mikveh* in Hebrew means 'concentration of water'). If this was quite impossible, it was permissible to collect rainwater. The bath itself consisted of a chamber about six metres (twenty feet) square, into which the water rose. A flight of steps within it provided access to the bath: in Friedburg, Germany, one has to descend seventy-seven steps before reaching the water. From a small room overlooking the bath, a woman supervised the correct performance of the ritual acts. The *mikveh* in Montpellier is situated below basement level, in a Romanesque vault dating from the seventh century AD. One can still see the changing-room with its stone benches against the walls, and the gemeled window overlooking an expanse of water the purity and stillness of which quite take your breath away.

Muslims, who require total bodily purification for the celebration of Friday prayers, have in similar fashion associated Koranic law with the practice of the hammam (or Turkish bath), which has become an occasion for meditation and spiritual as well as physical purification. The ablutions at the fountain that accompany each of the five daily prayers are performed as the prayers get under way, because, as the Sufi proverb states, 'cleanliness is a part of faith'.

In purifying body and soul, water also enables us to enter into another state of being. Since time immemorial, it has been regarded as a symbol of passage, marking the great milestones of life's journey: the bath after birth that is common to most civilizations, the ritual bath before marriage, and the bathing of the dead to purify the soul before the voyage to the hereafter.

It can also be used to celebrate the rhythm of the seasons. The Celts and Germanic tribes, for example, used to offer their thanks to nature for the gift of life-giving rain in spring by immersing themselves in large tubs of water infused with herbs and spring flowers. This was known as the May Bath. The custom has persisted as part of the celebrations for Midsummer Day, and, according to a proverb, a bath taken on this day is worth nine taken on any other.

In much the same way, water is also used in certain initiation rites. In the Middle Ages, for example, on the eve of being dubbed knight, and having spent the three previous nights in prayer and fasting, the young aspirant used to take a bath in a large tub of herb-scented hot water in order to 'emerge with no taint'. It was this rite of initiation that inspired Henry IV of England to create the Order of the Bath, to honour all the knights who had bathed with him on the night before his coronation in 1399.

RENAISSANCE ARTISTS frequently took their inspiration from mythology and legend. One of their favourite themes was Psyche at her toilet, showing the goddess after she has lost the love of Eros, who wanted to admire the beauty of her face. This monochrome stained-glass window (facing page), in the Musée de Condé at Chantilly, shows her in a circular bathtub (the same that appears in Titian's Diana at Her Bath) and surrounded by 'invisible voices'. It is they who pour the hot water and perfumed essences from a variety of pitchers and elaborately shaped ewers. Throughout the centuries, the bath has been used to mark the significant moments in a lifetime and the passing of the seasons. This illustration (above) for a medieval calendar represents the May Bath, fragrant with herbs and spring flowers. It celebrates the restoration of fertility to the Earth and, according to popular belief, to childless couples.

WATER: SYMBOL OF REGENERATION AND RENASCENCE

A symbol of purification and of passage in the religious context, water is also a symbol of regeneration and renewal in the secular sphere. Was it not in the sulphur springs of Thermopylae that Hercules recovered his strength?

In similar fashion, the vapour baths of the American Indians symbolized rebirth; they were the means of experiencing an altered state of being. Inside conical huts, the Indians used to build fires that they would cover with stones, and then sprinkle the hot stones with water mixed with purifying herbs, such as sage, citron or lavender. The construction of the hut itself was symbolic. Usually it had a roof of willow branches because of that tree's analgesic properties, and the number of the uprights and of the stones on the fire all had specific meanings. Before the ceremony, the hut was covered over with cloth, creating a semi-darkness that symbolized the return to Mother Earth, signifying security and protection. The hot vapour resulted in the shedding of sweat – water returned to Mother Earth, which gave her nourishment. When the door was opened, the steam rose up in the sky to the home of the Great Spirit.

In Western civilizations, it is usually the total immersion of the body that represents rebirth – a concept enshrined most fully in the symbolism of the bath. To plunge into water is to return, quite literally, to the source of life and even – since psychoanalysis – to life in the womb. You float in water knowing you are absolutely secure. You permit yourself a small moment of regression, of vulnerability almost, in order to attain a state of relaxation and regeneration.

And it is true: when you emerge from the bath you feel revived; you have a curious sense of being transformed into a new person. This is the phenomenon at the centre of the ancient Greek cult of Demeter, whose adherents plunged beneath the waves to emerge with a new name and a new life. This 'plunge into cool water' is what Gaston Bachelard calls the 'dream of renewal'. It performs the same function as the Fountain of Youth, whose fabled waters were said to have powers of rejuvenation. Today, we all have a Fountain of Youth in our homes in the form of

RE-CREATIONS OF the baths of antiquity in Hollywood films have provided us with many moments to savour: they supply the pretext for sets more notable for their magnificence than their historical accuracy and designed chiefly to dazzle their audiences. The stars, regal as empresses, perpetuate in their turn the myth of the bath, so maintaining their own legend. Cecil B. De Mille systematically included at least one bath scene in all his films. The Sign of the Cross *of 1932 (above) features scenes of Poppea bathing. It is believed that she used only asses' milk for her bath, and so the movie depicts the milking of the beasts, followed by the long transportation of the milk, first in containers on men's backs and finally down a channel into the bath, where the Empress, played by Claudette Colbert, reclines. By contrast, authenticity of ancient customs and decoration was claimed by Edward John Poynter (facing page) for his canvas* Diadumenos; *the full nudity and subject matter, inspired by the young ephebe sculpted by Polycleitus, caused some considerable controversy when the painting was exhibited at the Royal Academy in London in 1884.*

a shower or the tap on our washbasin. The running water invigorates us and we emerge clear-eyed and fresh-faced, more youthful in our own eyes and in the eyes of others.

The dream of being restored to health by water is often linked to the hope of being cured of an ailment. Even today, in central Italy, people collect pots of rainwater or morning dew in which to steep meadow flowers and fragrant plants overnight. In the morning they remove the flowers and bathe their eyes and hands with the water for two days in succession, in order to keep sickness at bay.

This practice is reminiscent of other, even more ancient, rituals. In prehistoric times, people worshipped magic springs and holy fountains. Later, sick people would be carried to hammams and saunas to seek a cure. In Greece, the healing properties of water have been known and prescribed as a remedy since the time of Hippocrates. In the second century BC, Asclepiades of Prusa went to Rome and founded a school of medicine that made considerable use of water cures. It is one of the reasons why the Romans, as well as building *thermae*, also built many spas on the site of natural springs, among them the famous baths of Baden-Baden in Germany and Bath in England.

Thermal springs have been popular throughout the ages. We know that Charlemagne went to Aix-la-Chapelle (Aachen); Henri IV of France to Aix-les-Bains; Montaigne went to Plombières, Baden-Baden and Bataglia; Anne of Austria to Forges-les-Eaux; Madame de

Sévigné to Vichy; Louis XIV of France to the Pyrenees; and Madame de Maintenon to Barèges. But it was in the nineteenth century, primarily because of the growth of the medical profession, that the fashion for cures at thermal springs and spas really took off, making centres for balneotherapy and hydrotherapy fashionable vacation spots for an elite whose leading light was the Empress Eugénie. Today, it is the symbolic, restorative power of water to which we respond, more or less unconsciously, when we choose to convalesce at thermal spas or thalassotherapy centres – or even when we decide to indulge in a good, hot bath.

And yet, in the course of the nineteenth century, cherished ancestral beliefs about water were swept aside by scientific and technological breakthroughs. In just a few decades, as Jean-Pierre Goubert has pointed out in *Conquête de l'eau*, water passed from being something sacred and of ritual significance to being 'hygienic': it became 'God or Nature's gift, an industrial product, marketed and standardized'. Yet, he adds, we should not believe that our new-found mastery of water has erased all its symbolic significance from our memories. For even if 'the fundamental principles of hygiene are supposed to be purely scientific, our relationship with water and the criteria for cleanliness are essentially cultural'. There are many influences on us: what is part of our past is also part of us. For certain, the water in which we bathe is not something that can ever be reduced to a mere chemical formula: H_2O.

SINCE TIME immemorial, spring water has been an object of reverence and pilgrimage. Whether endowed with magical or healing properties, or simply a source of refreshment, this 'living' running water has over the centuries come to symbolize many things, among them regeneration and purity, which correspond most closely to our needs in the modern world. Millions of Japanese, who are especially strong in their passion for water, spend hours bathing and showering in the thousands of naturally occurring hot and cold springs, for example the spring at Takagarawa (above). What could be more irresistible or more delightful than to splash clear water over your face in response to the inviting sound of a gushing fountain – especially when it is as charming as this one in the village of Beykoz (facing page), situated on the Asian bank of the Bosphorus in Turkey.

PUBLIC BATHS

AS WELL as appreciating the symbolic significance of water, men have for many thousands of years satisfied what Gaston Bachelard calls their 'primitive sensuality' by swimming in cool water as a form of relaxation, and prolonging its benefits by means of perfumed oils and massages. In distant Homeric times, we learn from the *Odyssey* that 'when the great Odysseus had bathed in the river and washed off his body the scum which clung to his back and the flat of his shoulders, when he had wiped his head of the brine from the barren sea, when he had bathed all, and anointed himself with oil, he put on clothes...'

The 'ancient pleasure of bathing', as Dominique Laty writes in *Histoire des bains*, has always been either public or private, involving either immersion in water or exposure to steam or hot air. In different eras and civilizations, one or other type of bath tended to be favoured, providing a sort of snapshot at a particular moment in history of the way the body was seen to relate to water, and the nature of personal hygiene. For example, up to the nineteenth century, communal and public baths were almost always vapour baths: 'restorative baths' that cleansed the body from within. (Municipal baths and showers were an invention of the early twentieth century.)

In his book *Mechanization Takes Command*, Siegfried Giedion provides a detailed account of the history of the vapour bath, the use of which almost always reflected a particular ideal, philosophy or religious precept. The first such baths occurred in prehistoric times, somewhere in the East. The 'recipe' is simple, which is why the technique has endured: inside a hut, one digs an open hearth in the ground and in it builds a fire of resinous wood, on which huge pebbles from the river are heated until red hot. Once enough heat has been produced, water is thrown on the stones to release steam, and the person installs himself in the cabin. The resulting vapour bath, which produces a dry heat, we will describe as a Russian bath. The invention spread slowly along four main routes. In around the sixth century BC, it arrived in Greece, where it became an established practice within the gymnasium precincts and was eventually transformed into the familiar thermal baths. It spread north to Russia and the Scandinavian countries, moved down into the Balkans and Germany in the thirteenth century, and also spread southwards into Asia Minor.

It was in the last region that the Muslims invented the steam bath or hammam, also known as a Moorish or Turkish bath. An amalgam of the vapour bath and the Roman thermal baths, it was introduced into Spain with the Moorish incursions of the seventh century, and then spread through Europe at the time of the Crusades. After the fall of Constantinople in 1453, the Ottoman Turks introduced it to the Balkans and Hungary.

The distinction between the two types of communal vapour baths (dry heat and humid heat) is preserved even today in the different bathing practices of the Nordic countries and the Arab world (see pages 171–99). At three periods in history the West tried and rejected the pleasures of the vapour bath: during the Roman Empire, in the Middle Ages and in the nineteenth century. The fact is, the vapour bath is more than just a bath: it is a state of mind. In its country of origin, a person would feel the weight of his cultural traditions pressing on his skin, an experience that cannot effectively be transplanted to other peoples and other places.

The Letter from Uriah *or* Bathsheba and Her Followers in the Bath *(page 16), by the Mannerist painter F. Di Cristofani Bigi (1482–1525), represents the Jewish ritual bath called the* mikveh; *it requires pure water flowing from a natural spring and was for that reason frequently installed in a basement, as is shown in this painting. Open-air springs provided delightful natural bathing spots, such as the one in the fresco of* Women Bathing *(page 17) by Bernardino Luini (1480–1532). The Renaissance painters took much of their inspiration from classical antiquity and set many allegorical scenes in ancient baths. In this detail (facing page) from the cycle of frescoes on the them of Psyche at the Palazzo del Te, after drawings by Giulio Romano (1499–1546), the bath in which Eros and Psyche are standing is in the ancient Greek and Roman form. In the nineteenth century it was the splendour of the baths and the mysteries of the harem that fascinated Westerners, as the details of the hookah, chains and barred window (above) suggest. This is the frontispiece to the first volume of an account of the public baths by Paul Cuisin, published in 1822 under the title* Les Bains de Paris.

THE INVENTION OF THE ART OF BATHING IN GREECE

The history of public baths begins in Greece in the sixth century BC, when they were associated with physical education. For the Greeks, bathing was not simply a matter of relaxing after muscular exertions, but of keeping mind and body in harmony. The first such baths were in the open air in the shade of olive trees, near the *palaestra* (gymnastic area) and *exedra* (place for philosophical disputation). They consisted of *louterions*: shallow, circular basins supported on pedestals at approximately hip-height. Women splashed water over themselves, while the male gymnasts washed before exercising and then cleaned off the sand in which they had previously coated their bodies to mop up the sweat of their exertions. For this purpose they employed a strigil, a small iron or bronze tool with a hollowed, curving blade.

Later, when the exercise area was transformed into a proper gymnasium, the baths were incorporated. In the fabulous site at Delphi, they comprise ten or more marble basins suspended at head-height, with lions' mouths above them, the whole enclosed within colonnades. Cascades of running water used to spill down onto the athletes' shoulders. A circular swimming pool with tiers of steps around the edge provided a place for the young men to sit and relax in the water before their lessons in philosophy.

Being associated with sport or military training, these were cold baths. Hot baths tended, in any case, to be disapproved of, unless prescribed by Hippocrates, for they were suspected of making the body soft and effeminate, while cold water made it fit for battle and tempered the character.

As physical training became a more important part of Athenian life, so the baths adjacent to the gymnasium became larger and more sophisticated. They acquired roofs and would typically contain

IN GREECE, before the advent of thermal baths, athletes bathed in the open air in an area near the gymnasium. They splashed themselves with water from louterions: *large basins supported on central pedestals. Bathing was mixed, as may be seen in the stamnos painted in circa 440 BC (above), which shows three women performing the eternally graceful gestures of bathing.*

bathtubs some twenty centimetres (eight inches) deep, the bottom of which gently sloped to help the water drain away. The Greeks used them rather in the way we use a footbath. Sitting on a little stool with the water up to their calves, they would trickle water over themselves with the aid of a scoop or sponge. Eventually, baths such as these were reserved for occasions when a person was particularly tired, and they were replaced by a type of large, round basin with a flat bottom, in which people would wash themselves down with the aid a sponge – more than somewhat reminiscent of the traditional nineteenth-century stand-up tub, both in respect of the shape of the basin and the manner of washing. For anything less than full body washes, there were smaller receptacles supported on tripods.

It was during the fourth century BC that bathing became an activity one could describe legitimately as an art. In that period, the gymnasia in every large city were built to a similar design. Shallow basins were hollowed out of the bare rock, and sometimes lined with clay tiles; in these, the young ephebes stood and splashed water over their bodies; the basins were arranged in a circle or parallel with the walls, depending on the shape of the room, and some of the deeper baths were reserved for therapeutic purposes. Niches were set into the walls, as a substitute for cloakrooms, and for part-body washes there were individual sinks, rectangular and of somewhat greater depth, fixed onto the wall and fed directly with water from a natural source.

The use of sand and oils eventually legitimized the practice of hot water baths, and the first vapour baths (using hot stones or white-hot iron bars) were introduced, installed in gloomy vaults lit only by a small top aperture. When the athletes had completed their exercises and removed the sand from their bodies with hot water, they would enter the vapour bath before going on to wash again with a kind of soap in a hot bath, and finally splash themselves down with cold water or plunge into the swimming pool; the whole process would be completed by rubbing in oils.

Hot water and hot air were thereafter an integral part of the Greek baths. Only the intellectuals castigated them, among them the Stoics and the writer Aristophanes, who tempered his criticism of the new fashion by the admission that hot water did at least reduce the burn of the razor on the skin! It was at this period that the first experimental hypocausts, circulating hot air under the floor, were constructed, and that an embryonic concern for aesthetics was combined with an aspiration towards comfort and well-being. The baths were decorated with mosaics, and the floors paved with pumice-stone so that people would not burn their feet; massages were also available after bathing.

In principle, people would bathe once a day (although some would go through the whole procedure several times in succession), either in mid-afternoon or before the evening meal. The baths thus became places for socializing, but – in spite of the allegations of abuse directed at the Sybarites – their chief function remained that of hygiene: they were designed for use after sport rather than for leisure. For the Greeks, pleasure resided elsewhere, in the narcissistic cultivation of the body beautiful, and in the desire to give pleasure and to feel a sense of physical well-being.

Warmth and conviviality were the principal elements that the Romans carried over from the Greek baths and incorporated, beneath ever higher and more luxurious cupolas, in their own thermal baths. For those were their pleasures, which corresponded most closely to their own desires and to the ethic of the Roman Empire.

In the fifth century BC, after training at the palaestra, the Greeks appreciated an invigorating shower quite as much as we do today. The vase decoration (above) depicts four athletes standing under streams of water gushing from four animal's heads. There is even a bar for hanging up clothes. One difference was the quality of the soap, which had none of the smoothness and fragrance of our own: it was made of saltpetre, ash and goat's fat.

BENEATH THE ELEGANT CUPOLAS OF THE ROMAN BATHS

Its thermal baths probably did as much as anything to make Rome eternal. For of all the ruins still to be seen in so many towns of the famous Roman Empire, the baths are the most impressive, demonstrating the exceptional level of sophistication the art of bathing had attained. Never again would such costly and luxurious installations be built.

The Romans had always adored water. Before the existence of purpose-built baths, they used to swim and dive in the bracing river currents and placid lakes. As in Greece, cold water was a symbol of health: it stimulated the body and proved the bathers' virility and austerity of character. In the first century AD, Seneca used to plunge into the icy waters of the Aqua Virgo on the first of January of every year. As he aged, he contented himself with the slightly less chilly waters of the river Tiber and finally made do with the warm water of his own bath. This led him to write that he was 'only one step away from sessions at the bath-house'.

The bath-houses, or *balneae*, were originally small, private commercial establishments, often financed by wealthy individuals; here the Romans first discovered the pleasures of alternate hot and cold baths on the Greek model. It was not until 19 BC, during the Republic, that Agrippa inaugurated a new era of public bathing with the completion, after six years of construction work, of the thermal baths, or *thermae* (a word of Greek origin meaning 'hot'). The building consisted of a vast rotunda twenty-five metres (eighty-two feet) in diameter, surrounded by other rooms. It was situated in a landscaped park with an artificial river and a lake for swimming. For the first time, water was brought directly to the baths via a purpose-built aqueduct and was heated by means of a hypocaust (a system for circulating hot air through passages under the floor, which was supported on brick piers, and later through flues inside the walls).

The Romans did not exercise their bodies in establishments such as these because they wanted to satisfy the requirements of some ideal of beauty, as was the case in Greece, but rather to safeguard their health, to keep clean and, most important of all, for the sheer pleasure of it. The space dedicated to bathing now took pride of place. Even though the *palaestra* was still present, physical education was more or less taken care of by a simple warm-up exercise designed to enhance the effect of heat and to raise a sweat. And as the centuries passed, even such exercises as these were replaced by a preliminary period in a room maintained at tepid heat. As for the

THE SAME graceful gesture is represented in this Graeco-Roman bas-relief of around 470 BC (above) of Venus emerging from the waters and by the woman bather (facing page) painted by Théodore Chassériau (1819–56) in a detail of his canvas of 1853 entitled The Tepidarium at Pompeii. *The warm-air room of the Roman baths, the* tepidarium *was an intermediate stage in the bathing procedure in which the body was accustomed to the heat and sweating by means of rubs performed by servants, before one moved on to the hot-air room, or caldarium. While the setting is authentic (and can still be seen in Pompeii even today), with its bronze charcoal-heated brazier and niches in the wall for storage of clothes, the atmosphere is redolent of the sensuality that was associated with Roman or Oriental baths in paintings right up to the end of the nineteenth century, as a means of circumventing the prevailing prudish morality.*

exedra, it ceased to be part of the entrance and developed into a separate complex, consisting of a club room and a library.

Thanks to the many extant literary sources, we can follow a typical Roman on his progress through the baths. He begins by leaving his clothes in a niche of the *apodyterium*, where they are looked after by a slave. He then passes into the warm-air room or *tepidarium*, where he can sit and relax and apply oil and ointments. He can then choose between the dry heat of the *laconicum*, where water is thrown onto heated pebbles so as to make the air breathable, and the humid heat of the *sudatorium*. He then progresses to the hottest room of all, the *caldarium*, its length one-and-a-half times its width. If he wishes to cool down, he can move into an alcove lit by a shaft of light from above, where he can splash himself with the cold water that gushes down into a vat called the *labrum*.

After his vapour bath, the bather enters a round alcove containing a pool capable of holding a dozen people, with steps down into it. There he sits on the second-to-last step, just like a Greek, and cleans his skin with the aid of a strigil, before rinsing himself with repeated splashes of water. In certain establishments, he may be provided with an individual bath. Finally, he moves on to the cold room, or *frigidarium*, where he plunges into the pool and enjoys the delights of frolicking in cool water. He can, if he wishes, return first to the warm room, in order to ease the transition.

A wealthy patrician would be accompanied by his slaves, one of whom would watch the cloakroom (thefts were common), while another would carry the phial of oil, the soda and the towels, and yet another would help him in and out of the baths or clear a path to the ever popular *labrum*, and finally scrape his skin with a strigil. If he did not have with him a slave skilled at massage or the removal of superfluous hair, then the patrician might avail himself of the services of the masseur on duty in the *unctorium*; the latter would settle him on a couch and efficiently perform a relaxing massage.

Over the years, many other amenities were added to the baths, making them something like a cross between an aquacentre and a theme park: there would be open-air pools, sports and games rooms (what might be called today 'fitness rooms'), gardens, porticoes and walks embellished with statues, 'bars', restaurants, relaxation rooms and, finally, cultural amenities such as libraries and theatres, where one could choose between plays, poetry readings, debates and concerts.

To set the scene and convey the hurly-burly atmosphere of the baths, we can do no better than to quote Seneca's *Moral Epistles*: 'I'm surrounded by the most terrible racket, my lodgings are right by the baths.... When the top gymnasts are training and swinging their lead dumb-bells, when they are labouring, or at any rate pretending to labour, I hear them groan; when they exhale, I hear whistling and rasping breath. And if I get some lazy bather who wants no more than a cheap massage, then I hear the sound of the hand slapping the shoulders – a different sound depending if it lands curved or flat. But if a ball-player arrives and starts keeping score, then I am really done for. And let us not leave out the picker of quarrels, the petty thief caught in the act, the man who is in love with the sound of his own voice in the bath. Nor should we forget the swimming pool and the mighty slap of water every time someone dives in ... and then, imagine the hair-plucker

THE POETIC nature of the baths at Herculaneum is summed up in this vestibule (above) with its peristyle and fine pedestal-basin: the scene that greeted bathers on their arrival. The balneae *were originally small private baths, often built by rich patricians, that charged for admission, but pressure from the authorities soon turned philanthropy into civic duty. (There were something like one thousand such baths in fourth-century Rome.) The intimate atmosphere of the* balneae *contrasts with the ostentation of the imperial* thermae, *the first example of which was built in AD 19, and to which water was carried by a special aqueduct before being heated by a system of hot air circulating under the floors and within the walls.*

who keeps up a perpetual falsetto yapping to attract attention, only silent when he is setting someone's armpits on fire and making another person cry out in his stead. Then there's the man selling drinks, with his sing-song cries, the sausage seller, the confectioner and all those cookshop boys, each with his own characteristic inflexion to cry his wares....'

Not only architects but emperors would compete to build ever higher domes and ever larger bays to house the windows of coloured glass that let the sunlight filter through and bathed the interior in soft light. As for the interior decor, it became increasingly sumptuous: columns of granite or porphyry, walls decorated with stucco and enamel panels and equipped with elaborately carved cornices, seats and basins with sculpted bases; underfoot, acres of white marble; mosaics everywhere, even on the bottoms of pools, with pictures of flora and fauna, and sea and river gods; and water, water everywhere, cascading in jets, pouring from silver taps, and so on.

This riot of luxury was intended for all to enjoy, without exception, for the baths were built with funds raised by the commune or State and were generally free. Unfortunately, it was not long before the authorities stepped in to bring them into line, the first to intervene being Nero. As Alain Malissard explains in his historical work *L'Eau et les Romains*, the building of public baths was seen by the Emperor as part of a concerted plan, on the part of the State, to govern by taking control of the people's pleasures. The Baths of Nero were built in Rome in AD 60. The building is vast, almost three thousand square

NO DOUBT the temperatures of 40° C (104° F) in the caldarium *at the Baths of the Forum in Pompeii (above) were made tolerable by the refreshing shade and the basin of cold water, or* labrum, *in an adjacent apse illuminated by an* oculus *or roof-shaft. These small baths built by wealthy patricians are in stark contrast to the elevation of the Baths of Diocletian (pages 26–27), shown in an imaginary recreation of 1880 by Edmond Paulin; this was a set exercise for students at the École Nationale des Beaux-Arts in Paris. One can almost imagine oneself strolling through the extravagant rooms, experiencing the excited atmosphere and perhaps meeting the wealthy freeman from Petronius's* Satyricon *in the* frigidarium: *'Trimalchio, absolutely streaming with perfumes, [who] had himself wiped down not with an ordinary cloth but with towels of the finest and softest wool, while three masseurs swigged Falernian [wine of Campania] under his nose.'*

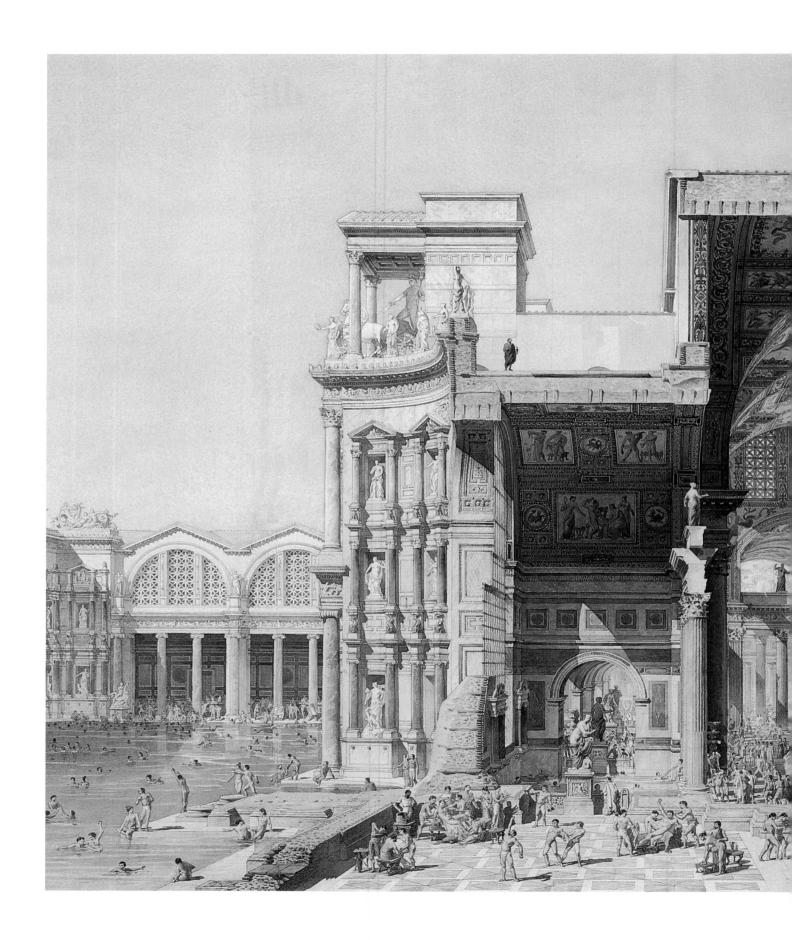

metres (thirty-two thousand square feet), and constructed according to the Emperor's original design, with a central aula, designed for one-way traffic and leading onto all the bathrooms, bringing the bather back at the cloakrooms near the entrance. This building plan, much employed subsequently, allowed for the installation of a separate entrance for women. Even taller and larger than that were the famous Baths of Caracalla, built around AD 217, which occupied 140,000 square metres (one and a half million square feet), while the baths constructed under Diocletian, which opened in AD 300, could accommodate over three thousand bathers in 150,000 square metres (one and a half million square feet).

These vast baths required water, and a lot of it, and Roman engineers were unmatched in their ability to channel it, convey it along aqueducts and store it in monumental cisterns (more than one hundred metres (three hundred and twenty feet) in length in Diocletian's reign); even the ruins that have survived to the present day leave us dumbfounded.

As we contemplate the sheer scale of their achievements, we may begin to wonder just why they built so many public baths. And, while we know it is true that they loved water and regarded hygiene as a noble ideal,

and would certainly have seen the baths as an antidote to their sedentary life and gargantuan banquets, what the *thermae* offered them, above all, was undoubtedly the opportunity for conviviality and spontaneous pleasure.

At the eighth hour in the Roman day, which today, depending on the season, would be four or five o'clock in the afternoon, a gong was sounded to signal the opening of the baths. On payment of a token sum each, the waiting crowd could enter the precincts. One would encounter there men and women (in spite of the fact that we have inherited an image of the baths as symbolically more masculine than feminine), as well as children; rich and poor; slaves; thieves; prostitutes; gymnasts; dandies; night watchmen; writers such as Pliny the Elder, dictating his impressions to his scribe; political figures; and even the emperor himself, accompanied by his retinue of guards and officers, testing his popularity and keeping himself in the public eye. One might admire the flamboyant turnout of a rich former slave, like the freeman described by Petronius in the *Satyricon*, who, 'absolutely streaming with perfumes, had himself wiped down not with an ordinary cloth but with towels of the finest and softest wool'.

UP TO the eve of the First World War, bathing scenes were the only way for painters of representing nudity without bringing down the wrath of the moral majority. Painters often turned to mythology and the baths of antiquity for their inspiration, as in one of the most accomplished canvases by the English painter Frederick, Lord Leighton (1830–96), The Bath of Psyche, *exhibited for the first time in 1889. In the detail (above), Psyche lets slip the last veil before entering the water, presumably as a prelude to an assignation with Eros – much like Ariane in Albert Cohen's novel* Belle de Seigneur, *before meeting Solal, wanting 'first, to make herself pure, to bathe, ... hopping with sheer joy, she ran to the bathroom'. A contemporary of Lord Leighton, Sir Lawrence Alma Tadema (1836–1912) was bold enough, in 1909 (facing page), to show slender young women fully naked in transparent water. As you contemplate the ivory whiteness of the bodies and their marble surroundings, in an atmosphere of serenity pitched somewhere between that of the Roman* thermae *and the hammam, if you let your eyes wander towards the entrance, you can pick out the niches in the cloakroom where the women sit and talk.*

And then there were all the hawkers and pedd-lars, each with his own distinct cry, and a whole world of spectacle – actors, storytellers, confidence tricksters and fortune-tellers. It was an extraordinary mixture, something like the hubbub of a large open square in modern Morocco, but translated to the setting of an imperial palace, all the delights of being part of a crowd, the opportunity to stand and stare, to do a bit of eavesdropping and swan about, plus – and it is not to be sneered at – the chance to keep snug and warm in winter in the most luxurious surroundings imaginable.

Such success was bound to have its detractors. Some attacked the waste of state funds or saw the whole system as a deliberate encouragement of idle-ness, a brutalization of the people. Others, mainly the Stoic philosophers, believed the hot water and use of perfumes were a sign that society was going 'soft'. Seneca once said that the Romans had an obsession with smelling good, but ended up washing 'to wash off their perfumes'. And it is true that the cult of the bath bordered on the neurotic or the absurd. Some people with nothing better to do would go through the procedure several times a day, and then go back to bathe at home – and that was just before dinner. At the start of the third century AD, although the baths traditionally closed at dusk, popular enthusiasm was such that the Emperor Cara-calla decided to leave them open all night. But of all the criticisms, the most frequent was one of moral

LYING BACK against silk cushions on a couch of opalescent marble draped with an animal skin, in the warm air of the Tepidarium *(above), painted in 1881 by Alma Tadema, this sublime beauty reclines languidly, all pink from the warmth of the* caldarium, *'sated with heat and pleasure'. She is the image of sensuality and lassitude, with scarcely the strength to support the weight of an ostrich feather or the embossed bronze strigil. Among the rare scenes of male bathers is this canvas (facing page) by the Mannerist painter Girolamo Macchietti (c.1535–92), which magnificently recreates the atmosphere of the baths at Pozzuoli, the famous thermal spa and bathing resort near Naples. The body is first scraped with strigils, then massaged and anointed with oils, the ancient implements for which (strigils, scoop and alabaster) are shown in the drawing (right).*

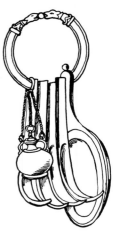

laxity, symbolized by nudity and the mixing of the sexes. The naked body, and the care lavished upon it, was the pointer to the class to which you belonged, and for a patrician, nudity in front of inferiors was of trifling importance. Mixing of the sexes was introduced in the reign of the Emperor Caracalla. Inevitably there were outbursts of licentious behaviour, which successive laws tried unsuccessfully to curb. Eventually women were forbidden access to the thermae by the Council of Laodicea in AD 320, and St John Chrysostom, Patriarch of Constantinople at the end of the fourth century, finally issued a total condemnation of the baths. For, since the start of the Christian era, it was not merely that the baths had a bad reputation, but their display of luxury hinted at materialism, and their condoning of nudity at an interest in the body that was tainted with sensuality and sin, both of these being vices that the Church fiercely condemned.

And yet, even in late antiquity the Romans were still constructing *thermae* in the furthest cities and provinces of the Roman Empire: Vienna, Trier, Badenweiller, Sanxay, Paris, Nîmes, Arles, Timgad,

Carthage and Volubilis. There were also numerous spas, among them thermal baths built over hot springs, which they held in particular affection, the most famous of which is in Bath, England.

The baths survived long after the fall of the Roman Empire, leading Alain Malissard to conclude that they were 'the fullest and most consensual expression of the Roman way of life'. And certainly it is true that the Romans' love of water was a legacy they passed on wherever they settled.

And yet, even if at the very heart of Christianity there were those such as Pope Gregory the Great, who, in AD 590, still permitted baths of short duration 'if luxury and sensual pleasure are not the motives for seeking them out', nevertheless, by an inexorable process in all the Romanized territories, baths were gradually abandoned. Poorly maintained, they ceased to function, until they were no more than witnesses to a lost technology. It was not until the Middle Ages, at the start of the eleventh century, that public baths resurfaced, and people were able to discover once again the delights of communal bathing in the medieval bathhouses.

EVERYWHERE THE Romans settled, they built thermal baths, evidence both of their love of water and their talent as builders. They were the pioneers of the spa. On the site of healing springs (whose efficacy had been recognized since the time of Aesculapius), the ruins of their baths may still be seen today. Emerald green water lapping against yellow stones is the image (facing page, top and bottom) one retains from the beautiful baths at Bath in England, where the water of the main spring emerges at a temperature of 45° C (113° F). The baths flourished for four centuries, and were later restored by monks in the twelfth century AD, but it was in the eighteenth century that the town attained the height of its popularity, acquiring its magnificent urban architecture as the baths came back into fashion. Where they could not rely on the miracle of natural springs, the Romans had to build gigantic aqueducts to supply the large thermae in the towns. In 1914, Zeno Diemer gave us an interpretation (above) of the Via Latina south of Rome, at the crossing point of the Aqua Marcia, Aqua Tepula, Aqua Claudia and Anio Novius.

The Gentle Warmth of the Medieval Bathhouse

Who among us has not been astonished to see those medieval miniatures with their scenes of public bathing: slender young women, stark naked but with elaborately coiffed hair, accompanied by men as naked as themselves, splashing about in baths of hot water and merrily tucking into a banquet on an improvised table made of a plank slung over the bath vats, covered with a linen runner?

The clear, warm water has been sprinkled with rose petals and a fragrant infusion of elderflower, rosemary, camomile and clover. After the love-feast in the bath, breaths are freshened by sucking liquorice or biting cardamom pods, and the delights of massage are enjoyed. The men choose to be shaved

or have their beards trimmed, the women to have their hair washed and anointed with oils redolent with musk, clove and nutmeg. Nor should we neglect to mention the option of hair removal, either by plucking with tweezers or with the aid of strips of cloth soaked in hot resin, followed by a rub with sweet-smelling essential oils.

The public bathhouses had reopened their doors. And with them, Western civilization rediscovered the delights of communal bathing. Let us try to understand why this happened. During the first Crusades, Westerners had been amazed to discover the sophistication of the Oriental baths that, in Byzantium, had survived the Roman Empire. Russian baths, the 'dry heat' baths originating in Russia and Asia, had spread as far as Germany – and in fact, in respect of the technique they employed, Western bathhouses were actually closer to Russian baths than to the Roman *thermae* or Turkish baths. As well as these foreign influences, there were other factors as well, such as the change in social mores – for it seemed that paying attention to the body no longer raised an outcry in Catholic circles – and the recognition of the importance of hygiene, thanks in particular to a work by the Persian philosopher-physician Avicenna called *The Canon of Medicine*. It was written in the early eleventh century and translated into Latin in the twelfth. Its prescription of alternating hot and cold baths, massage and gymnastics was widely adopted, indicating a renewal of interest in bodily fitness.

And finally, there was the growing awareness of self-hood, a phenomenon associated with the concepts of beauty and seduction in what was called 'courtly love': an off-shoot of the world of chivalry, that valued physical exercise in general, and jousting, swimming and bathing in particular.

In 1292, with just seventy thousand inhabitants, Paris was home to twenty-six bathhouses, called *étuves* or *hôtels de bains*. The memory of them lingers on even today in the names of certain streets in the fifth arrondissement and in the Marais.

From the twelfth century onwards, Western life began to acquire certain trappings of sophistication. There are many miniatures that show the rituals of the bath, indicating the attention paid not only to bodily hygiene, but to festivity and celebration. In the public bathhouses, people of both sexes bathed together in water infused with medicinal herbs. The manuscript Factorum ac Dictorum Memorabilium *by Valerius Maximus, illuminated for the Duke of Burgundy in circa 1470, illustrates (above) the delights of bathing* à deux *beneath an awning that could if desired be closed to keep in the steam, the pleasure prolonged with delicious food and white wine. Or one might prefer communal bathing (facing page) in a large bathtub with a tray across the middle covered with a linen runner, on which the food was set out. Naked but elaborately jewelled and coiffed, you could chatter away to your heart's content while the lutist played the latest courtly airs. The alcoves were for resting after the bath but, as we see, they also encouraged the amorous indiscretions that mixed bathing inevitably brought.*

landum etiam luxuria
malum cᷓ accusare
aliquᷓto facilius est
quᷓ vitur operi meo inserit· Non
quidem ut illi honorem recipiat
sed ut seipᷓm recognoscent ad
penitentiᷓm impelli possit· invitat
illi libido quᷓ eo hisdem vitiorum
principiᷓ oritur neqᷓ a reprehende

aut ab emendatione separent· geᵒ
mentie errore conexe· translateur
En ceste partie valerius commence
son vicᵉ livre qui est de vie z de
fais signes de memoire de la cite
de romme z des estrangiers· ouᷓl
apres ce que valerius ce viiiᵉ livre
precedent a determine de vertu z
operationᵉ vertueuses· en ce vi

These institutions generally comprised a room for hot baths, with, on one side, a large communal bath, and on the other, one or more bath vats capable of accommodating one or two people, for the use of the smarter clientele; these were made of wood and banded with iron. There was, in addition, a bathhouse with wooden tiers supplied with either dry or humid heat, from which the hot air escaped through holes in the dome above. The water was heated by huge furnaces in the basement and conveyed via wooden conduits. There was a room above supplied with couches and bedding, and sometimes perhaps a pint of cold white wine.

There are many prints that convey the atmosphere of these public baths, the most famous of which are probably those by Albrecht Dürer entitled *The Men's Bath* and *The Women's Bath*, as well as large numbers of miniatures depicting bathers in a hot water bath, with or without a bath sheet, singly, in pairs or in groups. Depending on whether the bathhouse keeper was also a barber, additional services might be available, such as cupping, massage, hair-removal, hairdressing, beard-trimming and even, in the case of the barber-surgeon, bleeding. There might also be hospitality: for example alcoves containing beds, and drinks and meals for consumption in the bath.

Everywhere in the West, places like these formed part of everyday life. In England, one particular establishment for male bathers had a Turk's head as its emblem, a reminder of the bath's origins; in Germany, the bathhouse keeper-cum-barber-surgeon advertised his services with a sign depicting a bundle of leafy branches (used to whip the body and promote the circulation, as in modern saunas). The baths were such a recognized element of daily life in Germany that *Badegeld* (bath money) was included in workers' salaries, and a tax raised on the takings

THIS MINIATURE of 1405 from the manuscript Bellifortis *by Konrad Kyeser (above) shows with touching precision the layout of the hot water and hot-air baths. The brick furnace heats the tank of water to produce steam, which is conveyed via a type of alembic to the baths. The woman's state of undress is in accordance with German custom. It was perfectly usual to go naked to the baths, or at least draped only in a sheet, as here. Later when a growing sense of modesty began to restrict nudity, the men wore drawers, the women a* Badehr, *a long shirt slit all the way down the sides.*

of these establishments was used to provide free baths for the destitute. The bathhouse was sometimes treated as an alternative tavern, and the travel expenses of Albrecht Dürer included an amount for baths, under the heading of entertainment. In his home town of Nuremberg, there was even a bathing song that declared that with 'wine for the inner man, water for the outer, we'll be content'.

There were also many public baths in the open air, often installed by springs or in rivers. Those at Baden were already famous. Michel de Montaigne noted in his *Journal*, as he set out for Italy via Switzerland: 'Baden, a small town with a separate township where the baths are situated ... alongside a river.... There are two or three public baths in the open air,

used only by the poor. Of the other sort there are many, these being enclosed within houses; [they are divided] into a number of private cells, walled and roofed, which you rent together with a bedchamber, the aforementioned cells being the finest and best equipped possible, with fresh supplies of hot water piped in for each bath.'

In Germany, the public baths were mixed, but men and women were separated by a low palisade or trellis punctuated by small windows, allowing for conversation or the partaking of meals. Nudity, however, was not always acceptable. Visiting Baden-Baden in the mid-fifteenth century, the Florentine Poggio Bracciolini described how the men wore short drawers and the women loose, low-necked

With a beautiful mountainous landscape in the background, this scene painted by Hans Bock in 1797 (above) represents the tranquil atmosphere of the open-air baths at the mineral springs of Loèche-les-Bains in Switzerland. The local red wine is flowing, and the sounds ring out of flutes, crumhorn, lute and children's voices. Apparently by some miracle this idyll has escaped the storms of protest that greeted mixed bathing and nudity during the Reformation. After 1548, bathers not wearing drawers or a cloth around the waist were liable to a heavy fine, or even more radical measures might be taken, as in Germany, where they might have their clothes confiscated.

it'. Sometimes an establishment would have its own jingle, anticipating modern advertising techniques: *C'est à l'image de Saint-Jame/ Où vont se baigner les femmes/ Et en estuves aller.* (At the bathhouse in the image of 'St Jame'/ To take their baths the women came.)

Where the point of the Roman *thermae* was to enjoy the water and the convivial atmosphere, the communal bath and the parade, the point of the medieval bathhouse was entertainment and festivity. According to the historian Philippe Perrot, the bathhouse appeared like a place of 'an ecstatic promiscuity, in which bodies pampered, plucked and perfumed by the diligent hand of the barber or his servant mingled boldly in the steam and hot water'.

It was also a place for indulging in forbidden pleasures. Many bathhouses served as trysting-places. The legally appointed closing time was nightfall, but that was soon widely disregarded and the regulations circumvented. On the eve of the days for female bathing, men would simply stay at the baths overnight until they reopened the next day. In *Flamenca*, the courtly romance that spread the fame of the thermal spa at Bourbon-l'Archambault, a jealous husband inspects every nook and cranny of the

wraps. Walking round the gallery above the woman's pool, the Italian threw down coins for the prettiest, so that when they bent to pick them up, their gowns gaped open revealing all their charms.

In France, at least in principle, men and women did not bathe together; a system based on the alternate days of the week operated, as in the hammams. Some baths indeed were solely for women, one example being Le Lion d'Argent in the present-day Rue Beaubourg.

At dawn, the chant of the bath assistant rang through the streets announcing that the baths were hot. Waving his rattle, he would trot out his usual patter, taking care to repeat that loose women, good-for-nothings and lepers were not admitted, and ending with the promise that 'the baths are hot, I swear

*A*MONG THE *most ancient open-air baths situated by thermal springs are those at Plombières in the Vosges (above, left), the delights of whose hot and cold waters are celebrated here in a print of 1553 by J.J. Hugelin. It was of these same baths that Montaigne wrote in 1580, at the beginning of his* Voyage en Italie*: 'There is a large main [bath] ... thirty-five paces long and fifteen wide ... places are ranged along the sides with hanging bars ...' Another type of bath to survive the Middle Ages was the vapour bath that had reached Germany via Eastern Europe. In this wood engraving (above, right) by Hans Sebald Beham (1500–50), the* Women's Bath *exactly resembles the modern-day Finnish sauna (see 'Private baths', pages 63–117), a disturbing illusion generated by the similarity of the room itself, the gestures, benches, wooden buckets and even the presence of children, to the saunas of today.*

baths, and keeps careful watch at the gate – but all to no avail as his wife's lover is there before him.

In the *Roman de la Rose*, the bathhouse is actually called the 'hotel of bounteous follies'; it is where the manservants and the young women go 'who enter the bathhouses and bathe together in vats'. The author, Jean de Meung, even makes so bold as to counsel the wife of a suspicious husband to make a tryst at the baths with her lover, and use the pretext of some indisposition to go there to take a steam bath.

This licentious behaviour in the bathhouses marked the beginning of the end for public bathing. The injunctions issued by the Church (Catholic and Reform) became more and more urgent, especially with the arrival of the great plagues and the spread of syphilis, which, owing to medical and scientific misinterpretations, gave water and hot baths a bad reputation. In France, as long as the plague was on the streets, the watchword was 'bathhouses and bathing, I beg you to shun them or you will die'. Condemned throughout the Western world, the public baths closed down one by one. In England the bathhouses were shut down by an order issued in the sixteenth century, in the reign of Henry VIII; they remained shut, or at least under very strict control, for almost one hundred and fifty years. It was the same in France, where their death knell was sounded in 1566 with the demand by the States-General of Orleans for the closure of all houses of prostitution, and therefore of the bathhouses in general. In Germany, there are indications of their continued existence up to the end of the sixteenth century, but by then times were beginning to change and one by one the towns closed down their baths. For almost two centuries, bathing was a forgotten pleasure.

The vapour bath, or so-called Russian bath, actually came to Russia from the north when it spread from Central Asia thousands of years ago. The prescription was simple but invariable: dry stones heated in a hearth and sprinkled with water to humidify the air. In the mid-eighteenth century, the Abbé Chappe d'Auteroche, visiting Siberia to observe an eclipse of Venus, was anything but convinced by his first experience. As he made to go in, he was so surprised by the clouds of steam that he thought there was a fire in the bath-chamber and closed the door again. Changing his mind, he undressed and at once broke out in a sweat. The intense heat went to his head and disorientated him, causing him to fall off his bench and break the thermometer that, as a good encyclopaedist, he had brought with him. The calm unhurried gestures of shared ablutions, the pleasures of massage, the opportunity for relaxation – these represent the opposite side of these baths in the canvas (above) by the Russian painter Letunov of The Women's Sauna, *a room heated by a large stove clad in glazed ceramic tiles.*

Two Hundred Years Without a Bath

To adapt the famous saying by Michelet, 'a thousand years without a bath'. When the bathhouses began to die out in the late Renaissance, so too did the use of water generally. Nudity, so widespread in the Middle Ages, became gradually less common, as Norbert Elias notes in *The Civilizing Process*. The ease with which people appeared naked before others had all but vanished, and with it the naturalness with which people performed acts of personal hygiene. Modesty thenceforth would have little to fear, as people chose in future to wash in privacy, and then rarely more than their face and hands.

What they did instead was dress up. And the more people resorted to artificial aids, the less care they took of their bodies. An article from the review *Le Mercure galant* of 1677 was unambiguous: 'Since being clean and tidy is no more than a matter of the appropriateness of a person's clothes ... we must, if we wish to be clean and tidy, suit our clothes to our size, condition and age. The law that we must indispensably observe, if we wish to be clean and tidy, is the law of fashion.'

The bathhouses disappeared, and with them the practice of communal and private bathing. By the start of Louis XIV of France's reign, there were just two public bathhouses officially recorded, and these specialized in therapeutic vapour baths prescribed by physicians, in the art of hair removal, and in amatory encounters. So it was that the opulent establishment of Monsieur Prudhomme was host to the secret assignations of the high society of the day, notably those of the cousin of Madame de Sévigné, the Comte de Bussy-Rabutin. Louis XIV presented himself at the establishment of another fashionable bathman, La Vienne, to have himself beautified on the occasion of his first amorous adventures. He rewarded him later with the position of senior *valet de chambre* at the château of Versailles. Such escapades were known as 'going to spend the night at the bathman's'. At the same time, one could avail oneself of the pleasures of a good bath, hair-removal, a haircut and beard trim, the application of cosmetics and a dinner washed down with fine wines, and even draughts of aphrodisiacs; and on top of all that, one was guaranteed absolute discretion.

In England, a century later, there were a few public baths in London offering a similar service. Casanova commented on them approvingly during a visit, noting that you could 'eat supper, bathe and stay on to sleep with a courtesan for only six guineas'.

As in the Middle Ages, these establishments were generally run by men who combined the functions of barber, bathman, bathhouse keeper, hairdresser and wig-dresser – professionals in the art of the bath – who in addition sold toilet and beauty products to their clients.

At the end of the seventeenth century, a few new bathhouses opened their doors, usually at the instigation of doctors like Nicolas de Blégny, who gave 'vaporous baths' near the Porte Saint-Antoine, Paris, in an establishment set in its own garden of medicinal plants; the patients were made to lie in hammocks above infusions of herbs! In 1678, it was Pierre Dionis, Surgeon-General to the Queen of France, who came up with the idea of 'Roman-style baths': 'the premises are laid out in a manner made agreeable and deeply satisfying to the eye by the urns, busts, basins, items of porcelain and paintings used to decorate them,' as described in *Le Mercure galant*.

For bathing fanatics, apart from the few bathhouses, there was still river bathing and the thermal spas. The latter were prescribed by doctors for purely therapeutic purposes, but that did not mean one could not also enjoy them. One who did so was Michel de Montaigne, who praised bathing as a salubrious practice and deplored the closure of the public bath houses.

In the following century, Louis XIII of France, Anne of Austria and Cardinal Richelieu went to Forges-les-Eaux, while Boileau and Madame de Sévigné loved to stay at Bourbon-l'Archambault, a spring equipped with Roman-style public pools and fashionable private 'showerbaths' in the basements of the royal residence. Louis XIV and Madame de Maintenon were soon to set the seal on the reputation of the sulphur baths at Barèges, while Baden-Baden in Germany and Bath in England continued to flourish.

River bathing won plaudits from members of the medical faculty everywhere for the invigorating and toning qualities of cold water. And if the people delighted in open-air bathing, so did the kings of France and their entourages. Henri IV was a fine swimmer who frequently bathed at Saint-Germain, accompanied by the Dauphin, the future Louis XIII. In summer, Anne of Austria and her attendants loved to disport themselves in the Seine, remaining there for several hours each day, dressed in long, loose shifts of coarse unbleached linen that bellied out in the water and preserved their modesty effectively. Even Louis XIV, whose dislike of water has no doubt been exaggerated, used to delight in repeating his childhood habit of swimming swiftly across the river Marne from one bank to the other, followed by the flock of courtesans who were obliged to copy all that he did.

The Parisians used to swim in the Seine – quite naked – between the Quai Saint-Bernard and the Quai de la Tournelle. It was such a popular activity that the authorities had to intervene on more than one occasion. Proper establishments for river bathing were then cautiously opened up. A married couple called the Villains provided changing-rooms of canvas-covered wooden planking, hiring out of shifts for women and towels for men, and bathing areas demarcated by tarpaulins suspended from posts in the water, with ropes stretched out as guide-lines. This initiative of 1688 marked the beginning of an unstoppable craze, leading eventually to the

FOR ALMOST two hundred years, from the end of the sixteenth century, bathing and its associated pleasures were frowned upon in the West, restricted to rare prescriptions for medicinal purposes. One by one the public bathhouses closed down, for moral reasons and because of repeated injunctions by the Church; at this period, water and frequent immersion was thought to be unhealthy and responsible for spreading plague and syphilis, and 'debilitating' body and soul. All that was left was swimming in rivers and ponds, as evidence of what Bachelard calls the 'primitive sensuality' or affinity that exists between fresh spring water (in particular) and the human body. This detail (above) of a painting of 1640 in oil on copper by Wolfgang Heimbach, entitled Young Girls after Bathing, *shows the moments of repose that follow the initial headlong rush to dive into the cool water, scattering shirts and shifts on the moss springing beneath bare feet.*

construction of proper swimming pools that, in the course of the eighteenth and nineteenth centuries, helped once again to 'domesticate' water and bathing and permit them to be regarded as a part of normal everyday life.

Around 1750, initially in aristocratic circles, water was cautiously reintroduced as an essential element of maintaining bodily hygiene, the first step in a process that would lead to a revival in public bathing. It was one of many indications since the start of the reign of Louis XV that a new image of the body had emerged. A different mood was in the air, first at court, then in the streets of Paris, and women began to turn away from artifice and to abandon constricting garments and skyscraper wigs. Gone was the arsenal of cosmetics; no longer was it obligatory to cake and conceal the skin with anything to hand; rather it was fashionable to let it breathe, to feel the air and water upon it, as well as the soap that was beginning to find favour.

This return to an emphasis on natural things and on physical exercise was justified by the new theories of the Enlightenment philosophers: Rousseau, Diderot and Voltaire in France, Locke in England and Basedow in Germany. There were also pronouncements from a growing number of doctors who believed in regular hot and cold baths, particularly since the discoveries of Lavoisier, who, in 1777, put forward his theory of respiratory exchange through the epidermis.

If Germany and England were rapidly won over, France required that 'someone of good breeding should want to use them and recognize them as fashionable, that being as powerful a motive upon us as

reason is upon our neighbours', as wrote that excellent psychologist Abbé Jacquin. He seems to have had his wishes answered at least to a degree, as the fops in Voltaire's *Le Mondain* take baths in order to 'be chic':

Un char commode, avec grâce orné
Sur le pavé le porte avec mollesse
Il court aux bains, les parfums les plus doux
Rendent sa peau plus fraîche et plus polie.

(A comfortable chariot, gracefully bedecked/ Bears him gently over the pavement/ He hastens to the baths, the sweetest perfumes/ Refresh and smooth his skin.)

Yet for these dandies and any new converts, public baths were few and far between. In Paris, there were no more than nine in 1773. The emphasis was primarily on medicinal water cures, although some establishments were luxuriously appointed. One such was the Bains Dionis, with its decor of flowers and exotic fruits, where you could indulge your senses after bathing with delicious snacks and improvised concerts. There were also the baths 'du Régent' in the Rue de Valois, originally designed for His Royal Highness the Duke of Orleans, which were comprehensively equipped with a bathroom containing bathtubs for full or partial immersion, vapour baths, a hot-air room and a shower room, and even 'apartments appropriate for receiving persons of the highest distinction'.

Establishments of this sort were to mushroom during the nineteenth century, many of them also equipped with swimming pools and bath cubicles.

THE EXTRAORDINARY GROWTH OF PUBLIC BATHS

For the provision of cleanliness and pleasure in the first third of the nineteenth century, there existed a staggering total of seventy-eight public baths in Paris alone. Following the opening of the Canal de l'Ourcq in 1837, as well as two new aqueducts between 1860 and 1870 that relieved the pressure on the river Seine, there were one hundred and twenty-five such establishments scattered throughout the capital, not counting the forty-five or so swimming pools.

For a description of these places, we can do no better than consult the guidebook by Paul Cuisin published in 1822. Invitingly subtitled *Le Neptune des Dames*, it was 'dedicated to the fair sex' and listed engagingly the best baths in Paris – and this at a period when some of the most famous had already opened their doors.

Starting at the Pont Neuf and proceeding along the riverside *quais*, with its distinctive chants of the bathing attendants, we come to the Vigier baths, founded by former senior bath attendant Poitevin and patronized by the lower middle classes. Facilities included more than two hundred baths for one or two persons as well as beds for relaxation. These baths benefited from a superb location on the river and were flooded with such bright light that the ladies bathing there had to pull their curtains to block out the sun, as well as to shield themselves from the 'idlers on the parapet [who] would not fail to take aim with their erotic eyeglasses'. The baths offer a wonderful view of the Hôtel de la Monnaie, the Louvre and the Quai Voltaire.

Beyond the Pont Royal, we find ourselves rubbing shoulders with 'the brilliant society of the Faubourg Saint-Germain'. The boats are elegant two-tiered frigates, whose 172 windows correspond to as many cabins with beds and baths. One would be greeted by charming maidservants. Distinguished food and fine wines, is that not a legend one has read before in some past century? The moment you enter, the splendours of the decor render you speechless: 'A gentle set of steps leads to sandy paths shaded by the parasol of a few poplars, and beyond that a rotunda for exercising horses. The path is filled with blossoms from tubs of orange trees, rosebushes, acacias, weeping willows, syringas, lilacs ... all of this in anticipation of the feelings of pleasure that lie ahead....' Here too the female clientele elected to occupy the cabins facing the quay rather than overlooking the Seine, the reason being a Peeping Tom on the river side with his eye glued to a telescope, who 'could count the lashes of your eyes'; he even used to write notes to some of them, eulogizing 'beautifully formed Venus, the foot of Atlanta, the breast of Hebe or the crescent of Diana'!

A little further downstream, even more sumptuous and lying anchored on the Left Bank, there was a 'superb vessel', once again trading under the Vigier sign, access to which was via a broad and majestic stairway, lit at night by a huge beacon and leading

THE MOST luxurious of the establishments trading as the Bains Vigier was moored beside the Quai d'Orsay. Access to the elegant Directoire-style vessel, illustrated above (left) and in the season-ticket announcement for 1807 (facing page), was via a broad and majestic stairway, lit at night by a beacon. On offer were 'baths for washing, for health purposes, or with bedrooms', provided by staff described as 'very fine-looking and elegantly turned out'. This meeting-place of the Parisian upper crust also counted among its clients the incroyables, *dandies and Royalists: gilded youths distinguished by the extravagance of their tailoring and affected manner of speaking without pronouncing their 'r's! Cultivating their eccentricity, they also frequented the cheap baths at the Rue de la Tannerie (above, right), showing off their bizarre behaviour to the curious Parisians.*

into an entrance hall decorated with a vast aviary; the service staff, male and female, 'most attractive, most neat and tidy and most flirtatious', offer baths for washing and for health purposes, and rooms with beds.

On the Right Bank, where the Rue de Bellechasse meets the Quai d'Orsay, we come to the finest establishment of its day, the Bains du Sieur Albert. It provided all the traditional services: showers – conventional, upwardly directed and combination – baths for washing and for hair removal, as well as Russian vapour baths and fumigation baths.

Paul Cuisin supplemented his guidebook with a list of much smaller but still 'charming' baths, such as the Bains Tivoli on the Rue de la Chaussée-d'Antin, set in spacious, landscaped gardens, with shrubberies where breakfast or tea may be consumed, and dotted about with small Chinese bridges and rooms for games of quoits, shooting, swings, shuttlecock and billiards. In the evenings there were fireworks displays. The speciality of the house was the nuptial bath, a curious sort of bath reserved exclusively for men that was aromatized 'with

foreign wines designed to fortify': a Hermitage wine for the chest and wine from Alicante. The bath itself was followed by a 'nutritious and hearty' collation: truffles cooked in champagne, syrup of veal bouillon, potato-flour bread and slices of leg of lamb cooked in tomato sauce. The fiancé then passed on to the cosmetics room where he was effectively marinated – 'enveloped in fine sponges, pads of cotton and scraps of flannel soaked with invigorating oils and essences made of spirits of musk and otto of roses'. Finally, he was anointed with lotions and massaged with Peruvian balm mixed with clove, vanilla, cinnamon, amber and a 'certain crushed insect' considered an aphrodisiac.

The author also paints a picture of the small Bains Montesquieu, with its magnificent linen, where one could sit in the garden and enjoy 'cups of chocolate as though it was raining chocolate, ... jellied caramel broth and truffles in gelatine cooked in Bordeaux wine'. He describes the establishment at the Rue du Mail, where there was a bathing gallery in a garden, and the baths themselves were extraordinary mixtures of cinnabar, lees of wine, tripe bouillon and

THE DEARTH of bathing establishments at the start of the eighteenth century did not mean that Parisians had to deprive themselves of water, as they still had the river Seine at their disposal. Gradually commercial baths were opened up that utilized the river, and then came the first bathing boats that filtered the river water. Moored alongside the banks, they reflected in their own particular fashion the society of Paris, becoming increasingly luxurious further downstream. The Bains Vigier just below the Pont Neuf, seen in this engraving (above) of 1830, 'accommodated the lower classes who just wanted to get the dirt off', while the vessel at the Pont Royal entertained the glittering society of the Faubourg Saint-Germain. In certain arrondissements with a plentiful water supply there were a number of smaller baths. At the Bains Saint-Jacques (facing page), tucked away behind grandiose gates amid green gardens, one was no doubt offered all the traditional pampering that follows a bath: massages and rubs with Macassar oil or the even more recherché 'huile des Abbés' or 'virgin's milk'!

bran-water – as well as the various showerbaths and the famous 'acoustic' bath for afflictions of the ear (simply a washing-out of the ears). On top of that there were beauty treatments that use the 'water of Sultanas', or the virgin milk of Ninon de Lenclos (a mildly depilatory lotion), or some sort of Mexican paste and oil from the Celebes.

Then there were the elegant Bains Chinois, formerly known as the Bains Orientaux, on the Boulevard des Italiens. Passers-by pause to stare at the extraordinary sweep of the façade decorated with Chinese porcelain figures, cut-out parasols and little bells everywhere. Of course, the only thing that is Chinese about these baths is their decor. As well as offering the freshest linen and all the pleasures associated with water, there was a café, a reading room, smoking room, etc. But its great boast was that it sold cosmetics and beauty products imported from Asia. One could be soaped with balsamic soap and take a 'dancing-girl's bath', armed with the reassurance 'that a pretty woman will emerge beautiful, a beautiful women ravishing, and that old age will shed a good twenty years...'.

This delightful stroll concludes at a magnificent establishment called the Thermes Parisiens, which opened a little later, in the 1850s. According to the brochure, one could enjoy the best mineral waters in an attractive salon, after relaxing in the various bathrooms, communal Russian baths, private hot-air rooms, or Turkish baths with Byzantine decor, massage rooms, relaxation rooms and a pool replenished with a constant supply of water from fountains gushing hot and cold! The interior decoration was of marble and mosaic set off by floral displays. The staff strived to outdo one another in diligence and discretion. The walls of the private bathrooms were clad in stucco, marble and glazed ceramics, the ordinary bathrooms were equipped with spacious baths for two, while those for 'combination baths' offered dry-heat vapour baths and fumigation baths, with sponge baths, showers and massage beds to follow.

This emphasis on luxury and physical pleasure as essential elements of personal hygiene contributed greatly to the success of the public baths, which were also aided by the rapid expansion of swimming pools during the same period.

In Le Paysan de Paris, *Louis Aragon stresses that there is 'a very strong link in the minds of men between baths and pleasure; this ancient notion adds to the mystery of these public establishments...'. It is an observation that would certainly have been true of the Bains Chinois on the Boulevard des Italiens, about which there was nothing Chinese except their decor (above). It was a sophisticated place, with exquisite hostesses and service staff, and was famous for the luxurious beauty treatments it offered, as well as the products it imported from Asia, such as the evocative and exotic 'Persian Water of the dancing girls', which promised to lend an eternal sparkle to the skin. Westerners were fascinated by the associations of Oriental baths and keen to experience for themselves the pleasures of the vapour bath. Indeed, in 1836, the establishment in question opened its own Turkish bath.*

THE NEW CRAZE OF SWIMMING POOLS

Of all the types of public bath, it was probably the 'cold baths' – the forerunners of the swimming pool – with their associations of play and activity, that were the most important contributing factor in the revival of public baths. For, quite apart from catering for basic bodily hygiene in the bathtubs of private cabins, baths of this type offered their heterogeneous clientele the enjoyment of water and the conviviality that in every century has been the prime motive for going to the baths.

Let us turn to the 'nocturnal walk' number 186 of Restif de La Bretonne's *Nuits de Paris* for a description of the primitive bathing areas that existed at the end of the eighteenth century. 'The first baths I saw were down some large steps, one on the Place Maubert bank, the other by Notre Dame or the Cité. These are baths for women. I continued on my way towards the island, and I saw baths above and below the Pont Marie with two big notices on the parapet, for men and for women. I continued my tour. I saw baths by the Port-aux-Blés for both sexes, I discovered others below the Pont Henri, opposite the Rue des Poulies, yet others on the Quai des Théatins; finally I saw some at the end of the Quai de l'Horloge, behind the Place Dauphine.... I returned to the Île Saint-Louis after the Pont Rouge ... without troubling myself overmuch about the men's baths, I passed the Rue de la Femme-sans-Tête; no one was making much noise, but, in the middle of the Pont Marie, I heard the sound of chattering from the women's bath. I went to a point opposite the Rue Poulletier; I leaned over the parapet and tried to overhear ... most of the young people were with their mother, a maid, an aunt or a neighbour.'

In 1761, upstream from these rudimentary baths, Jean-Poitevin, bathman by trade, took over a site on the Seine that looked across to the Tuileries. There he installed boats that pumped water from the river and distributed it to cabins that, as well as ordinary hot and cold baths and showers, provided vapour and fumigation baths. Twenty years later, a clever industrialist called Turquin fitted out two boats moored by the Pont de la Tournelle with cabins containing a total of twenty or more fixed bathtubs. These were suspended in the river and perforated with holes so that the current provided a steady flow of water. Each cabin contained three bathtubs, and linen was extra. He called his invention the Bains Chinois. Unfortunately he was accused by Poitevin of unfair competition and was obliged to close down. Early in the summer of 1785, he opened the first Parisian swimming pool that boasted its own school of swimming. This occupied an area demarcated by four boats and had a bottom made out of wooden slats. The following year his idea was copied by Deligny, who set up in business by the Quai d'Orsay. Swimming was the 'in' thing to do. Once it began, the craze was unstoppable, and bathing establishments with swimming pools sprang up everywhere.

In combining a hygienic function with enjoyment of the water, swimming baths helped to foster an enthusiasm for swimming that was supported by doctors and educationalists alike. The most famous school for women was the École Lambert, which opened its indoor pool on the Île Saint-Louis in 1838. In its day, it was quite the most fashionable place to be seen. Luxuriously appointed in an Orientalist

WITH THE reopening of the public baths, Westerners came once again to appreciate the forgotten sensation of water on skin. By far the most popular bathing institutions were those that included a swimming pool (above), enabling people to combine fun and games with the requirements of personal hygiene, which was then strongly encouraged. Learning to swim was the height of fashion, and even the children of the Duke of Orleans went to Turquin's for lessons. When the instructor pronounced one proficient, one was able to swim in the Seine. 'We used to swim in mid-river,' the Baron de Thiébault tells us in his Mémoires, *'from the royal gardens to the Place Louis XV, followed by a boat ... carrying our clothes. We had delicious lunches of little pies and cakes and small glasses of drink set out on barrels floating upside-down, round which we swam and helped ourselves to what we could.'*

style worthy of the canvases of Chassériau or Del-acroix, it was a sort of temple to femininity, wherein water nymphs (sublime, no doubt, and belonging to what a journalist writing in *L'Illustration* memorably called 'the aristocracy of money') reclined voluptuously on sofas and nibbled delicious morsels to the strains of sweet music.

But the most extraordinary of these places was undoubtedly the Gymnase Nautique des Champs-Élysées, which opened in the 1850s. It was set in a park amid gushing fountains, and we are lucky enough to have a print that records its quite remarkable interior decoration. The pool itself was in the shape of an elongated rectangle, with a small, landscaped island in the middle linked to either side by

means of pretty little bridges of carved timber. The water could be drained to create a vast hall. As in a theatre, there were two tiers of galleries on either side, and the boxes and balconies were sumptuously decked with curtains and drapes. The building was lit from above by a huge glass roof, with plants growing out of window-boxes. White shades could be hung up on days of hot sunshine. A billiard room, rooms for reading and conversation, beds and private bathrooms completed the attractions.

In his novel *Le Diable à Paris*, published in 1857, E. Briffault probably had these extraordinary surroundings in mind when he described an atmosphere uncannily like that of the Roman baths, in which, amid a deafening cacophony of voices and

1850 SAW THE opening in Paris of the fabulous Gymnase du Champs-Élysées, set amidst gardens with playing fountains. It rapidly became the most fashionable spot in the capital, where one could rub shoulders with a cosmopolitan crowd worthy of the Roman baths in their heyday. As well as a wonderful pool (above), there were rooms for billiards, reading, conversation and resting, and there were private bathing cubicles. A restaurant and café completed the amenities. Sometimes great Oriental celebrations were held, or 'nautical and hydraulic Venetian evenings', water tournaments with rowing and swimming competitions, regattas, trips in boats and skiffs, and concerts.

activities, 'some recline, some drape themselves in the ancient style in their bathrobes, or stand apart like tragedians rehearsing their lines or greet one another like Roman gossipmongers, while others listen to an orator; there are philosophers who lay down the law about the world, morality, industry and politics; journalists, poets empty of poetry and punsters; the raciness of the tales and confidences is undisguised, everyone is posing, some with ostentation, others with arrogance, and others without even knowing it.'

The more wealthy clientele, having whetted their appetite for bathing and for exercise in general, and always searching avidly for new experiences, began now to explore the seaside and renew their acquaintance with the spa towns. Water cures became luxury holidays and leisure opportunities. The Empress Eugénie set the trend during the Second Empire (1852–70). A golden age began for the spa towns, with their racecourses and casinos all part of the package. 'It's extraordinary, these resorts,' Guy de Maupassant was to write later. 'They are the only fairylands left on earth. More happens there in two months than does in a year in the rest of the world. You would almost think they are not mineral but enchanted springs.' People ventured to the coast and discovered the newly fashionable delights of sea, sun (though not suntans) and sand. Aware of the new passion, in which lay the seeds of their own downfall, certain proprietors of de luxe Paris baths and swimming pools had sea water imported via the Dieppe to Paris rail link, and even made sure there was fresh seafood on their tables. But the spell was broken.

It remains true that pools like these were crucial in enabling people to rediscover the sensation of water on the skin, so long forgotten. It was a formula that was readopted in Western countries at the beginning of the twentieth century, when the pressing requirement was baths for the mass population.

IT WAS a quite different atmosphere at the Hôtel Lambert (above), which opened in 1838 on the Île Saint-Louis. There, in an Oriental-style decor, one might encounter the most delightful daughters of 'the aristocracy of money', as it was dubbed by a journalist on L'Illustration. *Appropriately chaperoned and wearing swimming costumes in the height of fashion, they took their swimming lessons, and afterwards, fatigued by all the bathing and water games, reclined gracefully on silken sofas nibbling delicious morsels, to the strains of a small orchestra playing fashionable airs.*

THE FASCINATION OF ORIENTAL BATHS IN NINETEENTH-CENTURY LONDON, PARIS AND NEW YORK

The great rediscovery of the century was Oriental baths. Europeans had encountered vapour and steam baths on two previous occasions in their history – in the Roman baths and in the medieval bathhouses – and they discovered them anew in the nineteenth century.

Given the vogue for all things Russian, it is not surprising that Russian baths formed a part of these de luxe Oriental baths, and that a number of these establishments incorporated communal hot-air rooms or private cabins. But what the Europeans of the time really loved were the Moorish baths or steam baths, thereafter always known as Turkish baths. What fascinated Westerners was not the Eastern ritual that accompanied the acts of personal

hygiene so much as the closed quarters of the women's bath, that forbidden place where veils and skirts were discarded, and which carried with it distinct undertones of the harem. 'By a chance event that I will pass over in silence, I was fortunate enough to be the invisible witness to a women's bath,' began Debay as a preamble to his description of the women's bath in his *Hygiène de la beauté*, which was published in 1846.

The writings of Western visitors to the East during that period contained descriptions of the luxurious furnishings of these places, the sophistication of the bathing ritual and the euphoric state it induced. In 1832, Lamartine was in the Lebanon and in his *Bains de femmes* conjured up in the minimum of words the delicacy with which the fiancée's bath was performed: 'First there were steam baths, then baths for ablutions, then the women had perfumed and soap-scented water poured over them.'

Théophile Gautier travelled to Egypt in the 1850s, and he tells us how he felt after a bath and a massage,

MANY PAINTERS were among the great nineteenth-century travellers who discovered the incomparable delights of the Moorish bath, where the hours would melt away in voluptuous pleasure. The Orientalist painters loved the subject as a means of circumventing the prevailing puritanism of a period that rejected nudity, sensuality and indeed the whole notion of leisure. Languid poses and a scarcely veiled eroticism characterize this detail of The Turkish Bath *by Jean-Auguste-Dominique Ingres (above), while* The White Slave *in this painting by Lecomte de Noüy (facing page) pouts suggestively as she sits over the remains of her delicious feast. This is precisely the atmosphere described in 1717 by Lady Mary Wortley Montagu, the wife of the British ambassador in Constantinople: 'The first sofas were covered with cushions and rich carpets, on which sat the ladies ... some working, others drinking coffee or sherbet, and many negligently lying on their cushions, while their slaves ... were employed in braiding their hair in several pretty fancies.'*

as he lay limply in the rest room: 'I stayed there an hour roughly, in a sleepy reverie, taking coffee and frothy lemonade; and when I left, I felt so light, so fit, so supple, so well recovered from my fatigue that it seemed as if the angels of heaven were walking at my side!'

But the majority of the accounts we have come from European women whose husbands were posted to the East. The pioneers were English, and the main things that struck them, because of the habit of modesty ingrained in Western culture by religion and bourgeois morality, were the easy acceptance by women of nudity and intimate and pleasurable attention to the body, and a mixing of the social classes that would have been unthinkable in Europe. Lady Mary Wortley Montagu, wife of Britain's ambassador to Turkey, visited the public baths at Addrianople in 1717 (see 'The sensual delights of the bath', pages 171–99), and in 1839 Miss Julia Pardoe followed her example. She describes vividly how she

was initially hypnotized by the atmosphere, the pall of dense, sulphurous steam that almost suffocated her, the sharp, savage cries of the slaves echoing round the domes, the muffled laughter and whispered conversations of their mistresses. The overwhelming effect on her of nearly three hundred half-naked women, draped in fine linen so wet it clung to their bodies; busy slaves stripped to the waist, arms crossed, balancing on their heads piles of embroidered and fringed towels; groups of pretty girls laughing and chattering as they ate confectionery and drank iced fruit juice and lemonade; children playing together. And later, the women reclining on sofas as slaves enveloped them in warm linen, poured essences on their hair and sprinkled their face and hands with perfumed water, and so on.

The British were the first to attempt to import Oriental baths into Europe. The great pioneer was David Urquhart, a British diplomat posted to the Orient during the 1830s. Fascinated by the Oriental

THE PREVAILING fascination with the Orient, and the Turkish bath in particular, provided the inspiration for nudes both beautiful and realistic. Note the gesture of total abandonment as the woman places herself in the capable hands of the bath attendant, in **The Bath** *by Gérôme (facing page). The intrepid English traveller Miss Julia Pardoe tells us in a letter of 1839 that, after scrubbing the body, the maid would cover it in a sweet-smelling soapy froth, pour over floods of warm water and sprinkle on aromatic essences of jasmine, rose, orange flower and geranium. The canvas of 1883 by Debat-Ponsan entitled* **The Massage** *(above) beautifully conveys not only the secular ritual of the acts performed but also the authentic decor of the hammam, past and present. In these two paintings are featured marble surroundings, ornamental tiles, the wall fountain or round washstand with taps of gilded brass, and the embossed scoop used to gently rinse the body. Also the finishing touch: the big hot towels of fringed and embroidered cotton in which the body is wrapped after the massage.*

style of baths, he determined to make Moorish baths a part of English life, raising private donations in order to implement his scheme. It was actually he who gave them the name Turkish baths. It was the poorer classes he had chiefly in mind, as the provision for public baths for the masses was patchy in the extreme. Londoners at that time had little choice. They could either bathe in the river Thames, where the baths were primitive but at least very clean, or in one of the few mixed baths available, usually adjacent to a spring, which provided cold water only.

Some were very old, such as the Roman Spring Bath (late sixteenth century) where, much later, Charles Dickens would make David Copperfield take cold baths on numerous occasions.

David Urquhart pulled out all the arguments to win over his compatriots to the idea of the Turkish bath, but without much success. He did not have much more luck with the financiers, who provided backing for one establishment only, the Hammam: the architecture was authentic, with a hot-air room topped by the traditional dome, the dim light entering through small, star-

shaped pieces of coloured glass. The baths continued to operate in Jermyn Street, London, until the 1970s.

There were a number of other places in London that provided vapour baths, but the atmosphere was more like that of a comfortable English club, open to members only.

The type of bath so strenuously promoted by David Urquhart did, however, provide the model for installations throughout Europe and in America. In the nineteenth century, a number of Turkish baths opened their doors in Paris, among them that in the Rue du Temple which, Paul Cuisin assures us, combined 'Asiatic [sic] delights with high standards of

maintenance'. The decor relied heavily on glazed tiles in various colours, the furnishings consisted of soft couches draped with mosquito nets, and bathers used 'a simar for a bathrobe [what we would call today a djellaba], and a turban instead of a cotton cap'. An atmosphere of serenity prevailed, 'with the most exquisite Arabian perfumes wafted by delightful cassolettes'. The accessories, basins and ewers were gilded, and the baths were filled from silver swan's-head taps. The beauty treatment baths had 'eau des Odalisques' added to them, which 'transforms the water into a snow-white foam, gives sparkle to the flesh tints and blueness to the veins that run down the breasts'. The body would be anointed beforehand with 'virgin cream of Aspasia' and oil of Sybaris, or with a greasy paste that adhered to the skin and contracted in water, so that it 'gave the skin the softest glow and penetrated muscles, nerves and brain, offering transports of ecstasy and delight'. To all this was added the attentive service provided by an enthusiastic staff, like 'darling little automata'.

In the United States too, the authorities were convinced of the benefits of vapour baths. From 1850 onwards, they began to encourage their use by building Russian baths and hammams, with gymnasia that could be used for warm-ups before entering the sweat rooms and massages for relaxation afterwards.

In the years following the waves of immigration to the New World, these establishments grew in number. More than half were used by the Jewish population, who had emigrated from eastern Europe, and who maintained the religious and social traditions of the bath. That is how New York came to have sixty-two vapour baths in 1897, the best known being the Russian Turkish Baths on First Avenue.

A CENTRAL requirement of the Muslim religion is the full purification of the body before weekly prayers, which is why the ritual of the hammam is never performed in mixed company. Aladdin in The Thousand and One Nights, *who so longed to see the face of the princess that he hid behind the door, was one exception to this rule, as are the figures hiding behind a column in the canvas (above) by J.L. Vauzelle, painted in 1821. Perched on raised clogs (facing page), in order to protect themselves from the burning hot floors of the hammam, are the* Frankish Woman and Her Maidservant, *in a pastel drawing by Liotard executed in 1742. The ritual of the bath is complete and the woman is about to be served coffee. The scene echoes the words of Jean de Thévenot, one of the first travellers to the 'Levant' in the century of Louis XIV: 'Finally, shod in her wooden pattens ... the Turkish woman wraps round her a striped burnoose, red or blue, linen or silk, and passes into a room furnished with soft divans set out on daises, where she savours iced sherbet and perfumed coffee, accompanied with a cigarette.'*

FROM PUBLIC BATHS
TO PUBLIC SHOWERS

Out with delight, luxury and sensual pleasure – and in with hygiene and cleanliness. That was the new motto for the public authorities in the nineteenth century and the first thirty years of the twentieth. As private baths gained a hold in the homes of the bourgeoisie, so the public baths became places for the masses, dedicated to cleanliness and little else.

The mid-nineteenth century marked the appearance in England of public baths that combined baths with washhouses. This idea apparently originated in France, where a chemist called Jean-Baptiste Dumas had proposed a free or inexpensive service of this kind. The French government failed to adopt his idea, but it did not go unremarked in England.

The earliest British establishments of this sort opened in Liverpool, which had a large working-class population, and then in London, where the Lord Mayor sought to remedy the appalling shortage of inexpensive public baths by raising the funds to build the first such establishment, which comprised a wooden hut with washing stations and cubicles for cold-water baths. The second establishment was apparently a little more comfortable, with hot water provided for washing, one hundred and seven shower cubicles with a towel service, vapour baths and two swimming pools.

Despite the huge success of this enterprise, there were few public baths built. In 1865, London possessed one municipal bathtub per two thousand inhabitants, as well as rather larger numbers of vapour baths. Historians generally attribute the lack of success of the public baths in England to the English

WITH THE arrival of private bathrooms in wealthy households and the vogue for sea-bathing, swimming pools and public baths aimed at the upper levels of society closed their doors. Establishments offering water cures survived, as for example the Admiralsbad in Berlin, photographed in 1910 (facing page), where the calm atmosphere and fine Neo-classical architecture provided the ideal surroundings for bathers to enjoy the pleasures of good conversation after treatment. The emphasis was now on developing baths for the mass population, of the type shown in this exterior view of the vapour baths in Brick Lane, London, which were frequented by Russian immigrants (above, left). Germany was responsible for introducing communal showerbaths – known as the people's baths, because they were more practical, quicker and used less water than bathtubs. The scene in this German engraving (above, right) is far removed from the splendours of the Orient, even though the elaborate architecture and decorated arches try to foster just such an illusion.

tradition of washing in the privacy of the bedroom, and to the large number of private bathrooms that came into existence after the 1880s.

In Germany, the first public baths of this type appeared in 1855, based on the English model. The Schweinemarkt baths in Hamburg offered washing stations with hot water and sixty-five bathtubs. Here as elsewhere, facilities for bathing in first- and second-class private cubicles were introduced subsequently, as were swimming pools. The fact remained that with all these refinements it was simply beyond the means of the less well-off to pay regular visits. The entrance charges, which included soap and towels, were reduced, but they were still too high to win over the majority and make them regular customers. As in England, by the mid-nineteenth century the wealthier Germans were beginning to discover the convenience of private bathrooms.

In France, during the Second Empire and particularly during the long Third Republic, the story of public baths takes on the somewhat austere character of a public health campaign, when all notions of leisure or pleasure were eliminated in favour of basic education in elementary hygiene.

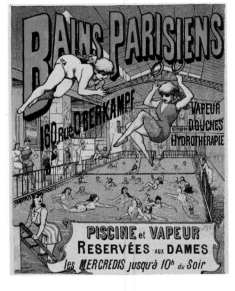

To win over the greatest possible number of converts, the first step was to make sure the prices at the public baths could be afforded by all. The newspaper cartoonists seized on the subject gleefully: 'I say Madame, is it true they're going to make everyone have their baths in public? ... Baptiste told me he read it in the paper.... But that would be indecent!' a little maid tells her mistress as she is about to climb into her portable bathtub.

By the dawn of the twentieth century, the bath had been replaced by the showerbath, henceforth regarded as 'the people's bath'. The idea of showers for the masses was born in Germany in the 1870s. In

France, the first municipal showerbaths opened in Bordeaux, then in the Rue de Belleville in Paris. They were an instant success: in 1903, there were 8,392 customers, a quarter of them women; by 1908, there were 153,285, half of them women. The municipal showerbaths seem to have successfully overcome women's reluctance to take off their clothes in public.

By 1900, public showers had become a working-class institution. In fact, it was only in the poorest areas that construction of showers continued, while elsewhere it was in decline. Then, having once permitted the public campaign to falter, the government of the Third Republic proceeded to overcompensate and continued to build new showers in even the tiniest villages right up to the eve of the Second World War.

In the United States, the history of the public baths followed a similar course. The first large-scale baths opened their doors in 1849 at 141 Mott Street, New York. The People's Bathing and Washing Establishment was open during the summer months. It consisted of a washhouse, a swimming pool and baths for men and women. However the prices proved prohibitive for the greater population, at whom these baths were aimed, and although at first there were six thousand customers a year, the baths closed down in 1861 for lack of regular business.

After the War of Secession (1861–65), the department of public works stepped in and in 1870 built the first floating baths, capitalizing, as previously in France and England, on the existing resource of the rivers. Large wooden structures on the Hudson and the East River, these pools were free and stayed open from June to October for the benefit of the working classes and the flood of new immigrants. In around 1888, fifteen baths attracted two and a half million

*THE ADVERTISEMENT extolling the virtues of the Bains Parisiens on the Rue Oberkampf (above) seems still to emphasize the fun side of bathing, but that was gradually to change in the first decade of the twentieth century with the introduction of the municipal showerbaths, intended for purely practical and hygienic purposes.
In* The Shower Bath *of 1911 by Albert Guillaume (facing page), the pretty girl in the mobcap has no inhibitions about offering her naked curves to the powerful jet of the showerbath at a thermal spa. Her experience is clearly the opposite of that endured by Madame de Sévigné in the seventeenth century at the hot springs in Vichy:
'Today I started having showerbaths; it is a fair imitation of purgatory. You are entirely naked in a little underground place which has in it a hose of this hot water which a woman plays anywhere one chooses.
This condition of retaining scarcely so much as a fig leaf in which to clothe oneself is something rather humiliating.'*

men and one and a half million women in a single year. They were intended to promote cleanliness and not to provide entertainment, and time spent in the water was restricted to twenty minutes.

Before the end of the century, public health experts launched a major crusade for cleanliness. Enlisting the help of the press, a powerful force in the United States, they demanded the establishment of proper baths that were free to the user. The physician Simon Baruch managed to raise funds from, among others, a philanthropic association dedicated to improving the living conditions of the poor. With that help, the so-called People's Baths were built in New York and opened their doors in the early years of the century. Over the entrance the legend was spelled out: 'Cleanliness Next to Godliness'. Colgate donated thirty-six kilos (eighty pounds) of soap. The building was made of concrete and metal and was equipped with showers (the people's bath once again, in North America as in Europe), and the costs for upkeep and running costs were kept to the minimum so that this time they represented excellent value for money, with towels and soap provided free. And yet, as the opportunities for bathing at home increased, so the use of the public baths declined. In 1914, plans to build the last of the public baths were scrapped. Others were closed down one by one. Following the Second World War, the majority were demolished, and the very last one closed its doors in the 1970s.

Everywhere in the West, the public baths were giving way to private bathrooms. In France, the large municipal shower-baths that flourished between the two World Wars have closed their doors, leaving little more to jog the memory than an evocative old sign over the doorway of a closed-up building, only

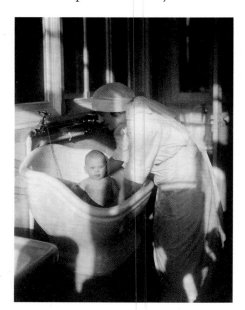

kept in good repair if the architecture was thought to be worth saving. Some of the installations with swimming pools have survived as witnesses to this past era, with their cubicles around the pool and the glass roof arching overhead. The best have been improved to meet modern standards, while others have been restored, their mosaics and empty pools diverted to a variety of uses. The Asser Levy Bath in New York was classified as an historical monument. It has recently been reopened after eight millions dollars' worth of reconstruction work. In France, one of the finest examples is in Roubaix, in the north of the country, where the swimming baths (a complex containing also bath and shower facilities) were built in 1932. The superb mosaics have been preserved, and, in time for the new millennium, the former pool will continue life as a museum of art and industry, with an information centre devoted to fashion and textiles.

With some being elevated to the status of museums, public baths would seem to have been relegated firmly to the past, along with the pleasures associated with them. But is that really the case? Not any more: in the major Western cities – New York, London, Geneva, Brussels, Amsterdam, and many in Germany – in response to changes in society, they are opening their doors once again, offering showers and baths at affordable prices or even for free. The purpose is to provide, for people living on the margins of society (almost like an attempt to duplicate in the secular sphere the role played by the monasteries since the Middle Ages), an opportunity for conviviality and social exchange that disappeared as bathing became almost exclusively a private matter in the second half of the twentieth century.

WHAT MORE beautiful than a child laughing in the bath. Happiness is a tub of water and a toy to float in it. Most crucial is the correct temperature of the water, lovingly prepared by the mother, as in that wonderful novel by Madeleine Bourdouxhe, La Femme de Gilles: *'It's time for the Saturday bath, I've got ready the big bowl, the water's heating up in the sun…. In the garden, Elisa leaned her beautiful heavy body towards the bowl; the water is just the right warmth, as far as one can tell. She plunged in her bare arms, and stayed a while like that, caught up in the softness of the water.' The time-honoured actions of the nurses, gentle and reassuring, are greeted by carefree smiles from the children in these photographs of kindergartens: above, in France in 1915, captured by Henri Manuel and, on the facing page, in Germany in 1925.*

PRIVATE BATHS

COMPARED with the variety, the exuberance and the sheer fun of communal bathing, taking a bath in a private bathroom may not sound too interesting. In the end it makes little difference whether you are soaking in a Minoan earthenware bathtub or a moulded acrylic shell, whether water streams over you from the shower or from a sponge bath in the tub, whether you rinse your hands by pouring water from a jug into a bowl or under the tap of a modern washbasin, for whatever the period, whatever the vocabulary, the actions performed and the basic equipment – technology apart – are very much the same, indeed all but identical.

No, the interest of the subject lies elsewhere, for our modern-day relationship with water, the well-being induced by the soft, foamy warmth of our daily bath, represents no more than the culmination of a complicated process of evolution. Over the centuries, that relationship has been at various times pleasurable or prohibited or sometimes simply a matter of necessity. Being bound up with attitudes towards the body and nudity, and the whole concept of modesty, it was at a certain point influenced by the phenomenon of increasing awareness of self and the cult of individuality, explored by Norbert Elias in *The Civilizing Process*, which necessitated the creation of the sort of private spaces that did not exist in houses before the first half of the eighteenth century. Then in the nineteenth century, as a distinction was progressively drawn between reception rooms and rooms for private use, the *cabinet de toilette* came into existence: the forerunner of the modern bathroom with running water.

THE ANCIENT MODEL OF THE MODERN BATHROOM

The model of the bathroom that took so long to perfect existed already – in almost complete form – among the ancient civilizations living around the Mediterranean. In Mari, Mesopotamia, more than two thousand years BC, the queen's apartments included an antechamber containing, it is believed, a sort of shower, followed by another larger room with niches to store clothes and bath utensils, furnaces to heat water, and two small, partly sunken baths: one for washing, the other for the pleasure of soaking the clean body in water delicately perfumed with oils. This general layout was adhered to right up to the eighteenth century, hence the plural form referred to in expressions such as 'appartements de bains' and 'suite of bathrooms'.

At Knossos, on the island of Crete, in the palace of King Minos built by the architect Daedalus around 1800 BC, the queen would have taken her bath in a room adjacent to her bedchamber, exactly like today. The walls of the room were painted with decorative friezes, as was the large, rectangular earthenware bath that is uncannily like that of today, being merely a little higher at the back. One can only wonder at the artistry, and the mastery of engineering that is suggested by the system of ceramic drainage pipes. Opposite the palace is the caravanserai, or inn, which has its own bathroom containing a number of earthenware baths, one of which is clearly portable judging by its handles; there is also

IN Woman at the Mirror *(page 62) of 1841, the Danish Romantic painter C.W. Eckersberg explores the bathing theme indirectly by representing his model with a towel round her waist, and her hand poised to let down her hair. In 1883, Degas'* Woman in the Bath Sponging Her Leg *(page 63), Impressionist in style, gives a much more literal account of the act of bathing. The imposing masculinity of the antique-style bathroom in the Palatine Gallery of the Palazzo Pitti in Florence, which was used by Napoleon for his daily hot bath (facing page), is in marked contrast to the fantasy of an overwhelmingly feminine world reproduced by so many painters. Not surprisingly, it is to women that are addressed the conventional sentiments of this poem written by Paul Cuisin in 1822, as an accompaniment to the frontispiece (above) of Volume II of* Les Bains de Paris ou le Neptune des Dames: *'O vous, sexes enchanteurs, ... esprits charmants/ Répandez vos faveurs sur nos bains salutaires/ A leurs flots caressants, confiez vos attraits/ Telles au point du jour, les fleurs printanières/ de la fraîche rosée aspirent les bienfaits.' (Oh you enchanting sex, you delightful spirits/ confer your favours upon our beneficent baths/ To their caressing waves, entrust your charms/ as spring flowers at the dawning of the day/ breathe in the goodness of fresh dew.)*

There is a delightful painting that shows what this bathing ritual may have been like between 1301 and 1235 BC. Queen Tiy, the mother of Rameses II, is seated in a partly sunken, shallow, oblong bath. Four servants surround her: the first pours the water, the second rubs her body, the third prepares her clothes and jewels, and the fourth, a supreme touch of luxury, presents her mistress with a sweet-smelling flower. This is not a bath in the full sense of the word, as water is no more than trickled over the body from elegant vessels.

In Homeric Greece, eight centuries before Christ, the bathing procedures echoed Egyptian practice. In the *Odyssey*, the poet describes how, when Odysseus arrived at the enchantress Circe's house, a woman brought in water in a large cauldron and built up the fire to heat the water, which whistled in the shining bronze vessel. Then, says Odysseus: 'I entered the bath, and, after cooling down the water in her big cauldron, she poured it over my head and shoulders to banish the sapping fatigue from my limbs. When she had bathed me and rubbed me with fine oil and clothed me in a handsome mantle and robe, she took me away....'

an inlet for running water, possibly even hot water. It is that simple fact – the ability to install an effective supply of running water – that is crucial to the development of the private bathroom, and for it to become a reality we have to wait until the beginning of the twentieth century. Which is why having a nice, hot bath remained for so long the privilege of those attended by servants.

In ancient Egypt, the elaborate palaces and dwellings of the Fayum all had their own baths. What the Egyptians called the 'lustration room' was adjacent to the bedchamber, and next to that was the anointing room, where they reclined on stone benches after bathing while a slave massaged them with oils and perfumed ointments.

Around the fifth century BC, private bathrooms existed in Greece. They were equipped in the same way as the public baths: shallow, rectangular bathtubs half sunk in the ground, built on the slope to allow the water to run away, or round bathtubs (uncannily reminiscent of the nineteenth-century tub), in which the bather stood or crouched in water that came up to his calves. There were shallow

THERE IS evidence of elaborate bathing rituals in the civilizations that lived around the Mediterranean several thousands of years ago, notably in Mari in Mesopotamia, where, more than two thousand years BC, the queen had a bathroom with stoves to heat water, and two small, half-sunken earthenware baths: one for washing, the other for rinsing – the practice adopted throughout the East. The same was presumably true of the palace of King Nestor, c.1200 BC (above, top) at Pylos in Greece. No people before us took such care of their bodies as the Greeks. There are scenes of people washing on many vases, as in this view of women at their ablutions on a fifth-century lecythus *(above). Théodore Reinach began building the Villa Kerylos at Cap-Martin in southern France in 1902, as a homage to the Greek way of life. The superb 'balneion', or private* thermae *(facing page), features an octagonal basin of veined Carrara marble. Not a trace of anachronistic modernism is visible: the taps are concealed beneath perforated metal covers, and the soap and sponge holders are adapted from sieves on display at the Museum of Naples.*

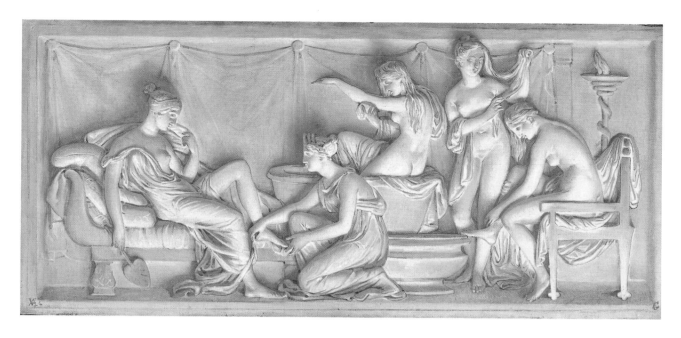

basins supported on tripods, or with handles, which were intended for splashing the body with water and for part-washing.

The ancient Romans did not possess private bathrooms worthy of the name. At best, there might be a small, dark room for part-washing, called the *lavatrina*, the ancestor of the modern *cabinet de toilette*. It was situated next to the kitchen because of the proximity to water – just like the earliest installations in the late nineteenth century. Water was stored in stone tanks, in cisterns or in reservoirs on the roof where rainwater collected. When the evening bath at the *thermae* became a daily event, morning preparations were somewhat perfunctory, according to the Latin poet Ausonius. 'Slave, up we get. Give me my shoes, my muslin mantle ... and pour me running water so I can wash my hands, my mouth and my eyes.' The pots and

bowls employed for such washes were normally made of earthenware and were most often used by women and children (they have frequently been found next to mirrors).

It was in the first century AD, when there were private aqueducts to supply the kitchens, fountains and pools of noblemen's villas, that private vapour baths first appeared. Pliny's villa in Tuscany had both a swimming pool by the colonnade, a *balneum* with bath-tubs, a well and a small pool. Later still, the *thermae* themselves were the models for private bathrooms. Patricians and wealthy freemen would typically have private bathrooms in their *domus* or villa, which they would use for parties. These were often as sumptuously decorated and furnished as the public baths (that they continued to patronize).

According to Seneca, 'you regard yourself as poor and

G.L. BULLEID chose an antique setting for his watercolour of 1907 of a woman preparing for her bath (facing page), with oil lamps, niches in the wall for flasks of oil and mirrors, and a mosaic surround suggesting the unseen bath. The title Binding the Fillet *describes the woman's action of tucking her hair into a band, and reflects the fact that in 1907 it was not usual to wash hair or even let it get wet.* Civilian Life in Athens *(above, top) is the theme of the grisaille painting by Nicolas Gosse and Auguste Vinchon. A Romantic interpretation of the subject of women washing, in the manner of a Roman bas-relief, it emphasizes the sensual gestures and clinging draperies of the women. The basin (above) is modelled on the Greek* louterion *and forms part of the furnishings at the Villa Kerylos.*

mean, if the walls of the baths do not glitter with large discs of inlaid marble, if the inlaid Numidian marbles are not set off by Alexandrian marbles, ... if the vault is not encased in glass, if the swimming pools are not clad in the marble of Thaos, formerly a rarity, if [filtered] water does not run from silver taps'. The freemen's baths are equally magnificent, if in a more traditional vein: 'So many statues, so many columns stuck there just for the sake of extravagance, for the decor.' There was rushing water everywhere, in a deafening cascade. The baths had enormous windows and were oriented so as to catch the sun throughout the day, enabling you to 'soak and tan your skin at the same time as you have a view from your bath over the countryside and out to sea.' Quite apart from being lavishly appointed, these bathrooms had running water supplied by private aqueducts.

The Romans took their passion for the baths with them to the outermost reaches of the Empire. Even as late as the fifth century AD, villas in Gaul and Germania were equipped with private bathrooms, and we know that Sidonius Apollinarus, Bishop of Clermont in AD 471, had at his disposal facilities for hot and perfumed baths, as well as a semi-circular bath and a pool. In Agde in Languedoc, southern France, there is a rather more modest Romano-Gallic villa, in which a small room with a water outlet in the middle of the floor can still be seen. Such an arrangement is common in modern bathrooms in Italy and other hot countries.

After the fall of the Western Roman Empire in 467, and the campaign against bathing launched by the Christian Church (even though, paradoxically, baths continued to exist in the monasteries over the centuries), the custom of bathing simply dwindled away. As with the public baths, it was not until the Middle Ages that the practice was revived.

ART IN THE Renaissance was much inspired by that of antiquity, and the fabulous stufetta, *or steam bath (facing page), in the Vatican apartments of Clement VII, who reigned as pope from 1523 to 1534, is no exception, for its frescoed walls are closely modelled on those of bathrooms in Pompeian villas. Whether this sumptuous room would have been intended more for therapeutic or for pleasurable purposes, at a time when the practice of bathing was anyway in decline, is debatable. Bathing the new-born child was a favourite medieval theme, and there are many nativity scenes showing that first symbolic immersion, notably of the Virgin Mary with the Holy Child. This detail (above) is part of a Byzantine fresco of 1265 in the Church of the Holy Trinity in Sopocani, Serbia. Note the gestures, moving in their simplicity, of the serving woman pouring hot water into the vessel to take the chill off the bathwater, having wrapped a cloth round the ewer so as not to burn herself, and of the Virgin testing the temperature of the water with her fingertip.*

MEDIEVAL BATHS

De bonnes herbes, elle fit bain ...
Puis mit l'eau chaude en la cuve,
Et drap dessus pour faire étuve.

(Of good herbs, she made a bath ... / Then put hot water in the tub/ and caught the steam with a sheet above.)

The bath of the Middle Ages is summed up in these three lines with their final emphatic rhyming couplet. There is not that much more to be said. One would take one's bath in the bedchamber, where a round wooden tub or vat with iron hoops would be installed for the purpose. Later, baths were taken in a separate room, the bathchamber, or even the 'bathing pavilion' that was sometimes built in the grounds of a château. But the ambience and the method of bathing were always the same.

Cleanliness or pleasure? It is hard to say. But it is certainly true that, within the private world of the aristocracy, there was a new enthusiasm for fitness and personal grooming. This focus on the body was common to all Western countries at this time, coinciding with a period of greater prosperity that encouraged individual expression and the development of a more sophisticated way of life. In Florence in the age of Dante (1265–1326), hair and body were washed once a week, while in the *Decameron* Boccaccio (1313–75) indicates that Saturday was the day for attending to bodily hygiene and for relaxation. In Italy, the new trend was encouraged by the availability of water in greater quantities and of better quality than in, say, France. There were public wells in the squares and at crossroads, public cisterns in Venice, underground canals, fountains and private wells. In Germany, the story was much the same, as we know from Konrad von Magenberg, author of the most well-known treatise of the day on the themes of medicine and morality, which recommends a regimen not unlike our own, based on a moderate diet, walks in the fresh air and frequent baths.

But whatever their motives – pleasure, beauty or cleanliness – lords 'in their private homes' got into the habit of 'drawing baths'. Usually people bathed naked, after a journey or after combat, or to dispel fatigue, but it could also be for pleasure. One might be alone, in a pair or in a group, for offering a bath was a form of ritual welcome. The writings of the period described the rediscovery of the bath, and the romance of courtly love gave it an important symbolic function, with a growing sense of eroticism characterizing the performance of such intimate acts under the scrutiny of another. Miniaturists, painters and engravers depicted baths and nudity so often that one might almost begin to think medieval people spent most of their time stewing in tubs full of fragrant herbs.

That the practice was widely indulged in there is no doubt, but it is very difficult to work out from individual cases what was the norm, in terms of the frequency with which baths were taken. John the Fearless, Duke of Burgundy, bathed about once every three weeks, while for another holder of that title, Philip the Good, it was about every four months, judging by the orders placed for wood for making bathtubs. Elizabeth of Bavaria, Queen of France, was no doubt even more assiduous, as there was a long-

As WESTERNERS returned home from the East after the first Crusades, they rediscovered a passion for baths forgotten since the fall of the Roman Empire. There are many scenes of bathing in the contemporary romances of courtly love and chivalry. When Tristan promised to rescue Isolde's honour, he swore by his bath:
'I will not bathe in hot water as long as my sword has not avenged me against those who did her ill.'
And in this fifteenth-century miniature (above) illustrating the romance of the knights Tristan and Lancelot, the armoured knight with his shield is bidding farewell to his wife as she sits peacefully in her bath, out in the open air, dressed as nature intended – the usual practice in the Middle Ages.

established tradition of Russian baths in her homeland, and we know that she always took two vats for bathing with her on her travels.

The vessel used for baths in the bedchamber was positioned near the fire where the water was heated. Round or oval in shape, and banded with metal hoops, it was made by a cooper in wood that would not rot: oak, chestnut or juniper. Once a sheet had been placed inside to protect against splinters, and an infusion of sweet-smelling plants added, all that remained was to climb in and wait for the maidservant to sprinkle on rose petals. To transform the bath into a steam bath was a simple matter of attach-

ing a linen sheet to a canopy, pulling it round the vat and trapping the steam that rose from the hot water.

By trawling through the account books of the period it is possible to explore the changing material culture of the bathroom. For washing hands, a wall fountain was used, of the type frequently depicted in works such as Dürer's *The Life of the Virgin*, where it appears beside a wall-mounted rail with a long, fringed linen towel. For intermediate washes between baths, the ever-present jug and basin were pressed into service. There were also basins with matching ewers filled with perfumed water, which would be offered to guests to freshen their hands: a

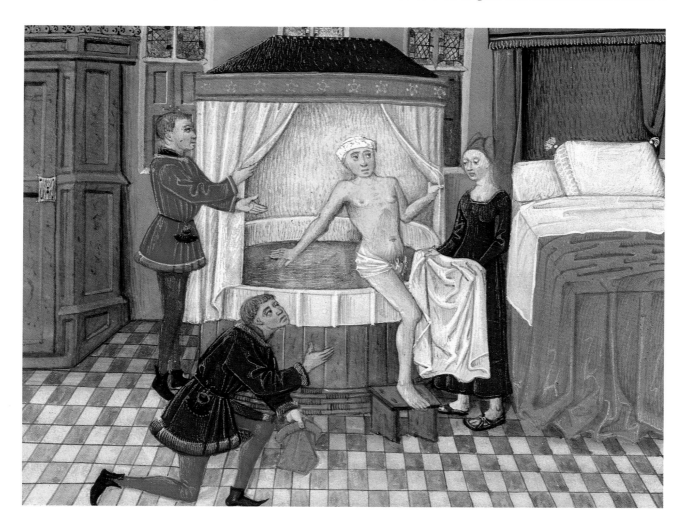

THIS ATTRACTIVELY decorated wooden bath vat is lined with a sheet as a protection against splinters and there is an overhead canopy with curtains to trap the steam rising from the hot water. The miniature (above) is taken from the illuminated manuscript of Factorum ac Dictorum Memorabilium *by Valerius Maximus, prepared in 1470 for Antoine, Duke of Burgundy. As he emerges from the bath, the lord is ministered to in the traditional manner by young servants, and prepares to wrap himself in the long towel presented to him by the maid of honour. Charles the Bold, the last to bear the title Duke of Burgundy and reputed to be a man of taste, was apparently the possessor of a silver bath that he took with him even when he went into battle.*

traditional sign of welcome for people invited to dine at one's home. The ritual was so taken for granted that to omit or refuse it was regarded as a calculated insult. The same was true of offering baths to the poor or to passing pilgrims, a practice that continued in the monasteries right up to the Middle Ages. In his book *Clean and Decent*, Lawrence Wright notes the presence in 1256 in a wardrobe room of Westminster Palace, London, of silver basins, apparently used specifically for washing the head. Basins of this type tended to be larger and with steeper sides, more like a prototype of the traditional tub, and they would be made of metal, often copper, and polished inside so as to serve as a mirror. One would stand the basin on matting or wooden slats and then, by kneeling down and bending the head over it, one could splash water over oneself and wash not only the hair but also the upper part of the body.

The wooden bathing vat was joined before long by the earliest metal baths, hammered into shape by smiths. There were even some made of silver, such as the one that belonged to Charles the Bold, from which he was never separated, even on the battlefield.

Over the same period, there were improvements in ways of heating water. For example, the bathtub could be connected by means of a pipe to a cauldron set over a small wood- or charcoal-burning stove. Later, the portable stove would be placed directly underneath the metal bath, and then one would take care to place a wooden plank inside to prevent the bather being burned by the hot metal. Anne of Brittany possessed a bath of this type.

Not only the equipment but the surroundings changed. A room dedicated to bathing, with a wooden boarded floor, was installed next to the bedchamber: it was known as the 'chambre d'estuve' or 'vapour bath chamber'. In such a room, in 1472, Edward IV of England prepared two bathtubs covered with linen cloths to welcome the ambassador of the Duke of Burgundy. In aristocratic dwellings, suites of bathrooms would soon be installed, known in France as 'baigneries'; these were usually situated on the ground floor, for the ease of obtaining a supply of water, and comprised at least one bathroom and a vapour bath.

At Westminster Palace in London, the royal quarters were equipped from an early date with fixed baths connected to tanks of hot and cold water. In 1275, water flowed from four gilt-bronze taps in the shape of a leopard's head. In 1325, glazed tiles were put up in the bathroom, and in 1351 a certain Robert was asked to supply two large bronze taps to supply hot and cold water for the bathtub of King Edward III.

Equally stylish was the late-fourteenth-century bathroom of the Hôtel Saint-Paul, on the ground floor of the Parisian palace of Charles V of France: it was paved all over with lias, a very fine-grained limestone, panelled in Irish wood and fitted with a door made of forged iron in the form of a trellis. Baths were taken in wooden vats bound with hoops set with gilt-copper studs, surmounted with a carved canopy.

THE THEME *of Bathsheba in her bath surprised by David is magnificently translated to a medieval setting in this masterly composition by Hans Memling of c.1482 (above). With her high forehead, hair pulled back and swathed in a turban, the slender-figured Bathsheba adopts a hieratic pose as she emerges from the bath, draped chastely in a manner that befits her nature. In marked contrast is the flirtatious pair in the preparatory sketch by Albrecht Altdorfer (facing page, bottom), a detail for his frescoes at the Imperial Baths in Regensburg. With its improvised canopy, a simpler form of bath characterizes this fresco of* The Married Couple's Bath *executed by Memmo de Filipuccio in the mid-sixteenth century. The scene is the familiar showing the maidservant who brings hot water and waits nearby with the towel and, in the background, the room where bathers may rest after their exertions.*

Baths in French châteaux were often installed in separate 'bathing pavilions', sumptuous places that were the scene of major festivities, very much in the grand tradition of the visitors' baths that used to be laid on for guests before a meal as a sign of hospitality. Eventually these events expanded into veritable water-banquets. For the aristocracy, the feast 'aux bains' became a fashionable form of entertainment. Guests were privileged not only to dine but also to bathe in the company of people such as Monsignor de Rovestaing, Monsignor de Bourbon, the son of the Comte de Russye and many other great lords, knights and squires, as was the case in 1462 on the estate of the Duke of Burgundy. Royalty was also welcome, and so, in September 1467, as the guest of the Provost-in-Chief, Louis XI of France found himself offered three 'sumptuously ornamented' baths.

It will be clear by now that 'taking a bath' had become more what the historian Georges Vigarello has dubbed a 'playful distraction' than an exercise in cleanliness. Decline had set in; in the elaborate bathing suites built in the early sixteenth century, people paid more attention to the decor than to their bodies.

In 1527, Philip of Cleves, for example, was the owner of a bathroom with four bath vats. These were surrounded 'by curtains and canopies of white Millau cloth, decorated with fringes, gilded knobs and five escutcheons bearing the heraldic device of the said seigneur'. The room also contained a bed, dresser and table, and eight small benches that one could use to sit on inside the bath vats; there were magnificent paintings on the walls. The adjacent hot-air room must have been very elegant, with all its shades of white. It was hung with fringed white linen curtains, and there were benches draped with white cloths and down pillows covered in fustian; underfoot there was a large muslin carpet worked in pale grey wool, together with four smaller ones. The furnace room next door served as a lodging for the servant who dispensed the baths.

Three years later, at the château of Fontainebleau, Francis I of France embarked on the construction of an extraordinary suite of bathrooms, which has now sadly disappeared. Out went the round wooden vats and metal tubs, and in their place the first proper oblong marble bathtubs were installed. The suite was on the ground floor of the main part of the chateau, and comprised two rooms for vapour baths – both hot air and steam – with tubs and baths, one bathroom with a large central pool surrounded by a balustrade and several smaller rooms in which one could relax while contemplating a *Mary Magdalen* by Titian or Leonardo da Vinci's famous *Mona Lisa*.

In Germany, Philip II of Baden installed premises no less desirable. On the ground floor of his castle was a large bath, lined with a sheet of tin, that was entered by descending five steps. It was surrounded by benches for the bathers' use and, given its capacity, was probably supplied by a thermal spring, The water was stored in a reservoir in the room next door, and was diverted in one direction to fill the swimming pool and in the other to a small room used as a vapour bath.

AT LEEDS CASTLE in England there is a sensitive contemporary reconstruction in medieval style of the bathroom of Catherine de Valois in the early fifteenth century (above). Note the gemeled window looking out over the outside world, the cushions, a blazing open fire to undress by and to heat water, the wooden buckets and large bathtub equipped with long strips of white damask cloth with a small repeat design, used to transform a hot bath into a vapour bath infused with herbs. On the table are towels and the ewer and basin for minor ablutions – this was used mainly for washing the hands before meals and could be quite a costly item, perhaps in chased silver ('moult bien doré') or enamelled around the edges 'with little roses and French coats of arms', like that of Charles V towards the end of the fifteenth century. In summer, it was quite usual for baths to be taken outside in the château grounds, in a tank fed by a spring. This tapestry from Tours (facing) of a château on the banks of the Loire represents a typically relaxed Renaissance scene, against a 'millefiori' background.

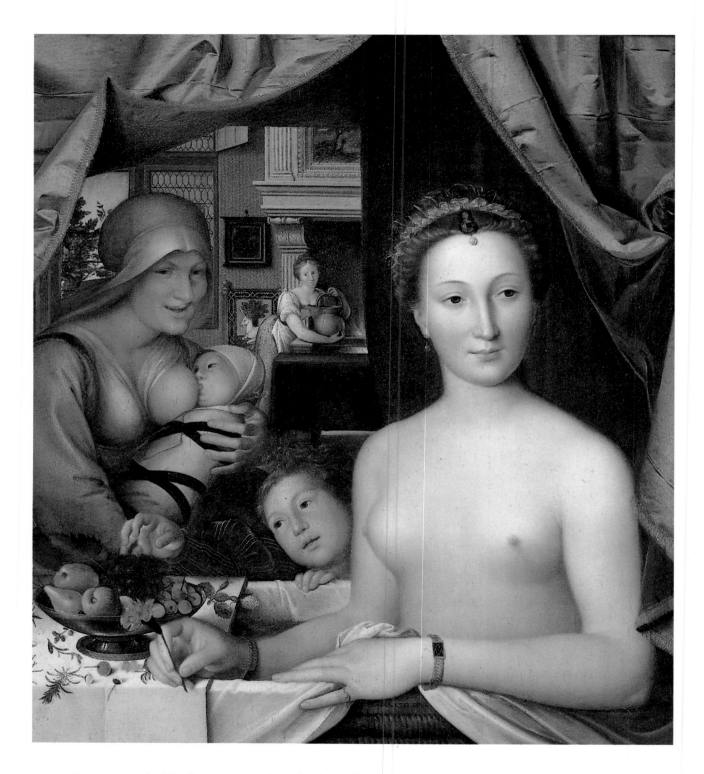

BEFORE BEING *hidden for centuries, the splendours of female nudity were celebrated in the bath scenes*
painted by members of the school of Fontainebleau. Diane of Poitiers, the mistress of Henri II, who started her day
with a cold bath, Gabrielle d'Estrées, favourite of Henri IV, with her sister, and a number of other anonymous
beauties were among those who enchanted the late Renaissance in delightful paintings illustrating the final days
of a golden era. In the seventeenth century baths disappeared, and with them nude paintings. Small, high breasts
and an icy sensuality characterize the Woman in Her Bath *by François Clouet of c. 1570 (above). She is eating fruit*
while seated in a bath draped with the traditional sheet, the silk curtains pulled aside. In the background are the
wet-nurse suckling a child and the maidservant taking a cauldron of hot water from the high stone hearth.
Nudity is resplendent, on the other hand, in the elegant and expansive gestures (facing page) of this
voluptuous Venus at Her Bath *who contemplates her beauty in an embossed mirror, in a detail from*
a painting of the school of Fontainebleau.

In Italy, dukes and prelates tended to favour bathrooms in the ancient style. The *stufetta* or small vapour bath used by Pope Leo X, born Giovanni dei Medici, was an exact reconstruction of one in a villa dating back to Roman times. In Castel Sant'Angelo in Rome, the vapour bath used by Clement VII is decorated with fresco paintings, and the bathtub, built into an alcove, receives its supply of hot water from a tap in the shape of a young woman. As one of his contemporaries wrote, when the Pope took his bath, he probably 'touched it with great resignation'. Where the dukes of Mantua held court, in Giulio Romano's masterpiece the Palazzo del Te, there is a tiny *stufetta* literally covered in frescoes, which can still be visited today: it comprises a small, square room with Corinthian columns, giving onto a small vapour bath with a domed apse clad, Renaissance fashion, in stucco encrusted with shells. Engravings convey more powerfully than any description these moments of pleasure and repose. In about 1530, Salviata depicted a charming scene of four naked women in a bathroom with a tall ceramic stove in one corner, niches for the elegant ewers, a stone bath draped with a sheet, a small pool where a seated woman washes her feet, the corner of a swimming pool and, in the background, a bed on which to rest.

In spite of all these amenities, the latter half of the sixteenth century saw the development throughout Europe of a growing aversion not only to baths but to water in general, which would soon be good for little more than to fill the basins of fountains and keep the jets of water playing. It was all superficial, purely for the sake of appearances – like the perfunctory washing of hands and face. Farewell the elaborate and silky hairstyles, farewell too, alas, the recipes for baths that would make the skin clear and soft and smooth and fragrant, just by using this ointment or that new cream from Italy.

True, voices were raised in favour of baths. In his *Essays*, Montaigne declares: 'In general I think bathing salubrious and believe we incur a small detriment to our health for having lost this custom common to most nations and persisting in many, that of washing one's body every day, and I cannot imagine it does much for us to keep our members dirty and our pores blocked with filth.' In her *Instruction pour les jeunes dames, par la mère et la fille d'alliance* (1597), Marie de Romieu stresses: 'I desire a good-looking girl to wash all over and very often in water in which good scents have been boiled up, for there is nothing so certain as that what makes a woman's beauty blossom is cleanliness.'

And yet it was to no avail, bathing went out of fashion. For almost two centuries, people were happy to 'wash' without water. Believing the absorption of sweat was a form of washing, they used instead to make frequent changes of linen. Baths in the bedchamber were for purely therapeutic purposes, ordered by doctors who took care to remove any lingering pleasure by prescribing a preliminary diet and subsequent bleeding and bed rest.

Once baths had become mere medical treatments, they ceased to be of interest to painters, and in consequence nudity disappeared from art. It was not until Watteau, Boucher and Pater, born around the dawn of the eighteenth century, that artists rediscovered this form of inspiration, as women rediscovered the luxury of a warm bath. In the meantime, the favoured subject was the woman at her *toilette*, or dressing table, putting the more public finishing touches to her fairly minimal preparation.

EXPRESSING ALL the sensuous delight of water, this little cameo (facing page, bottom) of Susannah in Her Bath, *a jewel of the Renaissance owned by the Medici family, was executed not long before bathing fell into a decline. In the seventeenth century, doctors formally advised against baths for healthy people, but that did not stop the wealthy owners of châteaux vying with one another to possess the most opulent* appartements de bains. *The apartment installed by the Archduke Ferdinand Maximilian at the Neues Schloss in Baden-Baden (above) is a Baroque masterpiece, while the curious 'bathing pavilion' of the Elector of Bavaria at the Nymphenburg in Munich (facing page, top), completed in 1721, took the form of a deep basin decorated with Delft tiles, overlooked on all four sides by a gallery where one could stand to watch the bathers. It led into a formal salon, a games room and a room for rest and relaxation.*

The Decline of Magnificent Bathrooms in the Seventeenth Century

In the seventeenth century, taking a bath was simply not the done thing. The prevailing fashion was for what sociologist Georges Vigarello called in his book *Le Propre et le sale* 'the courtesan's dry toilette'. Body rubs replaced the bath, and face and hands were wiped with napkins moistened with perfume. There was also the incomparable linen underclothing, 'kept the whitest in all the world'.

Although this new fashion in grooming may seem to us a retrograde step in terms of cleanliness, it is nevertheless true that for those who had the means to afford a fine linen shirt, the use of linen underclothing represented a real advance, protecting both the body and the outer clothing. And though water was no longer in direct contact with the skin, it was at least used regularly to wash the items with which it was in contact.

Around the mid-seventeenth century, an aristocrat would change his linen every day, compared with every three to seven days in the wealthy urban population. Instead of purchasing a bathtub, a person might splash out on thirty or more chemises or shirts, and that would be equally true whether one were a courtesan, Molière or the Provost of Anjou. The doctor Louis Savot made all this very clear in 1624: 'We can more conveniently do without baths than the ancients, because of our usage of linen, which today serves to keep the body clean more conveniently than the baths and vapour baths of the ancients could do, who lacked the usage and convenience of linen.'

The entire medical body threw its weight against water and the practice of bathing. To its reputation of allowing the vital forces to escape and letting in miasmas, was added the quite unprovable accusation that it encouraged epilepsy and dropsy. The Church, of course, was firmly set against bodily temptations of any description, and therefore recommended only a brief rinse of mouth and hands.

A change of shirt, a wipe of the face and hands, hair combed and powdered (the forerunner of the dry shampoo?), or, later in the century, covered over with a wig; scented powders and coloured make-up to hide behind, perfume (a deodorant before its time) to drench oneself in, scented sachets to slip under the armpits or into the folds of dresses; all the above stratagems illustrate perfectly the meaning of cleanliness in the seventeenth century. In the French dictionaries of the day, *propreté* was defined as being decent and seemly.

This toilette, or beauty regime as we might call it today, was all about presentation. It was a spectacle, like a play to which intimates and lovers were invited, with seduction as the major attraction, acting its part through reflections glimpsed in the dressing-table mirror. There are numerous prints and pictures of the period showing this morning scene being enacted before a piece of furniture swathed in lacy frills, later muslin, a combination of dressing-table and washstand.

Intimate personal hygiene was relegated to a small room in the wings called the *garde-robe*, or wardrobe, which began to appear next to the bedroom. The ancestor of the *cabinet de toilette* of the nineteenth century, it was a private place for intimate ablutions and for storing the associated paraphernalia, before architects had provided a special room for that purpose. For with the habit of bathing lost, bathrooms and bath vessels had long since disappeared from Parisian dwellings. The number of private houses with bathrooms could be counted on the fingers of one hand.

In the French royal palaces, *appartements de bains* (the name used until the end of the reign of Louis XIV) continued to be installed – large and magnificent rooms as elaborate as they were pointless. The taps for hot and cold water set above the bathtubs did not in fact supply running water: instead there were two tanks installed directly above the bathroom, the one for hot water set over a wood-burning fire, which the servants would fill every morning with water from buckets.

Particularly lavish *appartements de bains* were installed for Anne of Austria in the Palais du Louvre

by Lemercier, at the request of Louis XIII. There was a description of them in *Le Mercure galant*: '...with two vaults supported on marble columns, the only colours you can see in the place are azure and gold. All around there are portraits of the House of Austria (painted by Velázquez), with a few mirrors above them, and in the background a bathtub of white marble, into which hot water enters from outside through taps. The floor is of flowers carved from different woods.'

During the reign of Louis XIV, ostentatious installations such as these were intended to dazzle the courtesans and promote the glorious reputation of the Sun King. The external manifestations of the same desire were the fountains and jets of the water gardens, with their highly sophisticated plumbing

THE WOMAN *at her toilette is a common theme in seventeenth-century art. The woman is usually shown fully dressed and seated at her* toilette, *a sort of dressing-table covered in lacy frills with a mirror on the top, where she would perform minor ablutions in the presence of a favoured few. The real work of washing was done in secret in the* garde-robe. *In a century in which bathing and nudity were no longer familiar sights, even a glimpse of a deliciously bared calf could create a stir. The captivated gaze of the gentleman (above) is the proof of it, in this engraving of c. 1690 by Bonnart. In the same period, the Duchesse de Mazarin was said to have insisted on washing her feet while staying at the Couvent des Visitandines. The sisters refused point blank, whereupon she emptied out a big wooden box and filled it with water. It immediately began to leak and caused a flood.*

systems. The new symbolic function of water was principally to impress, and that is one of the reasons why, at Versailles and other châteaux, one suite of bathrooms was no sooner completed than Louis XIV was already planning another, yet more sumptuous, replacement.

The many splendours of the château of Vaux-le-Vicomte, which was built for his minister Fouquet, and in particular a certain bathroom with a rotunda, had rendered the King speechless with jealousy. He poached the architect responsible, Le Vau, for his own programme of improvements at Versailles. In particular, he asked him to replace the fine suite of bathrooms installed on the ground floor by his father with a sumptuous set of *appartements* comprising

five rooms: two antechambers, an octagonal salon, a bathroom and a room for relaxation. The result is a giddying assortment of pilasters and marble panels, presided over by two bathtubs of white marble, their two bronze taps mounted on the wall, together with a vast mirror and statues on pedestals.

Fixed bathtubs were of marble. The sunken bath installed by Louis XIV at Versailles is a true marvel. Octagonal and made of pink marble, it cost the State the sum of 15,000 *livres*. As it was three metres and thirty centimetres (eleven feet) wide and one metre (three feet) deep, it was necessary for the room to be enlarged and a new floor of coloured marble laid, as well as the paintings and gold leaf of the wooden panels in the ceiling restored. Later, Louis

In the seventeenth century, this anonymous print (above) would have been regarded as highly unusual, since it depicts chocolate drinking in association with bathing. The bath is more or less circular and made of metal with a moulded pattern, like a larger version of a basin used for washing. The bath sheet is edged with lace, as too is the bathing chemise worn by the woman, who poses with a mocking complicity. The hot and cold water flows from taps, giving the illusion of running water, although it comes in fact from tanks in the room above that need to be filled with pails of water by the servants. The hot-water tank would be heated by means of a wood-burning stove placed underneath.

XV presented the pink marble bath to Madame de Pompadour. Not without difficulty, she had it transported to the garden of her little house, the Hermitage. It had to be put onto rollers by a system of levers, and required twenty-six men, several metres of rope, vast scaffolds and a convenient window to effect the transfer. Today it has pride of place next to the entrance to the Orangery at Versailles.

Lavish bathrooms were being built everywhere. Around 1700, a large bathroom was installed at Chatsworth House in England, its walls clad in blue-veined white marble. The bath itself, half-sunken and made of marble, was deep and spacious enough for two people, and was entered by descending steps. Unusually, it had hot and cold taps. At the same period, in Holland, the director of the South Sea Company had a bathing pavilion clad in Delft tiles, on the top of which was a water tower and a room containing the machinery to keep the water circulating! In Germany, when the castle of Schwetzingen was given a Versailles-style makeover, a quite extraordinary bathroom was installed, its walls embellished with panels of white stucco decorated with reliefs of nymphs and bordered with amethysts. The floor is of pink and black marble, and there is a sort of stucco dais, imitating

draperies, that surrounds the sunken marble bath, access to which is via three steps. The water enters the bath through the mouths of eight snakes coiled round its edge. And what can possibly be said of the antique-style bathroom in the Prince's Apartments of the Palazzo Pitti in Florence (1754), with its inordinately high ceiling, and coloured marble floor, which would be impossible to heat during the cold Florentine winters but quite magnificent, with its Neo-classical frescoes and bath set into a large alcove.

The cold splendour of marble and grandiloquent decor: that was the style adopted during the *grand siècle*. But from the reign of Louis XV of France onwards, a new sensibility began to stake its claim. When the private apartments at Versailles were refurbished, small *cabinets de bains* were included in the plans. These attractive, intimate spaces provided for bathrooms with wood-panelled walls equipped with bathtubs of tinned copper, a room for relaxation and a water-closet 'à l'anglaise'. They were not 'appartements de bains' but 'cabinets de bains', the name by which they were known throughout the eighteenth century. What more ideal surroundings could there be in which to rediscover the private pleasures of the bath?

AT VERSAILLES, there were apparently more than one hundred baths in the courtesans' quarters, possibly of the type shown in this engraving by Bonnart (above) entitled Woman Preparing to Enter the Bath. *The round bathtub is surmounted by a magnificent brocade canopy and curtain, and the bath sheet embellished with a broad band of costly lace insert. No doubt then that this is the era of Louis XIV of France, and the bathroom is worthy of a duchess. As the print dates from the seventeenth century, when baths were mostly for medicinal purposes, we may suppose that the bewigged gentleman is offering some sovereign remedy designed to dispel the lovesickness with which the woman seems afflicted – or perhaps he hopes to fan her ardour! The daily bath taken by Marie-Antoinette was more austere. She wore a long flannel chemise and was waited on by just one chambermaid, while her bath sheet was made of cotton dimity, which had replaced costly cambric and lace.*

The Intimacy of the Eighteenth-century *Cabinets de Bains*

The Sun King died in 1715, and with him a whole world disappeared. After a century dedicated to reason, rigidity and etiquette, characterized by the triumph of outward appearance and the negation of the body, there was a return to naturalness, sensitivity and intimacy. Imperceptibly, the outward mask dissolved, so that eventually the real flesh-and-blood person and his private personality were 'no longer hidden behind paint and powder or conventional manners', writes Anne Marnhac in *Femmes au bain*. Already, at the start of the eighteenth century, there was a hint of the heady perfume of early Romanticism, which would foster an emphasis on the individual and favour the growth of narcissism. Louis XV was the archetype of the new sensibility: greater intimacy, simpler court etiquette, a more relaxed style in clothes, flounced skirts, lighter fabrics and simpler hairstyles. It was the return of the natural, and equally the return of Nature, which, during the Enlightenment, was seen as an entity of which the human being was an integral part. Also, there were intimations of a new and healthier lifestyle based on physical exercise and cleansing baths.

With the revival of bathing came the chance to rediscover ancient pleasures. At Versailles, Queen Marie Leszczynska had three *cabinets de bains* fitted out in quick succession, the last of which (still in existence) introduced the grey-blue and white wooden panelling that was to became the height of

fashion under Louis XVI. As for Louis XV, he had his *cabinets de bains* completely refitted four times.

Of the seven *cabinets de bains* in the royal family's private apartments at Versailles, the finest, the jewel of them all, occupies a small room approximately fifteen square metres (one hundred and sixty square feet); it is clad in grey panelling and decorated with medallions sculpted by the Rousseau brothers, which are overlaid with three colours of gold leaf: yellow gold, red gold and green gold. The medallions depict sporting activities associated with water (fishing, duck-shooting, children diving, men learning to swim, women bathing). On the panels of the internal shutters are illustrations of all the various bathroom accessories – combs, scissors, scent-bottles, sachets of powder, shaving-dishes, etc. – framed inside an interwoven design of rushes and dolphins.

All these *cabinets de toilette* gave onto the Cour aux Cerfs (an important technical detail, given the need for cesspools). There was one exception: the last bathroom built for Marie-Antoinette, on the ground floor of the Cour Royale, which was completed only months before the Revolution. Designed by Mique, it consists of a single, beautiful, almost square room, decorated with blue and white panelling, with two windows giving onto an English-style courtyard containing a cherry tree; in addition there was a fireplace, a bath, a couch and upholstered chairs by Jacob; next door was a small room with chairs and lit by a window overlooking the bathroom. The ultimate touch of discreet luxury is provided by the panels sculpted by the Rousseau brothers, the frames of which bear illustrations of aquatic flora and fauna and of bathroom accessories, in an intricate design of ribbons and flowers.

WOMAN AT HER TOILETTE is *the familiar title for this rather unusual engraving by Boilly (above), which shows a young woman absorbed in the task of washing herself, while sitting astride a new item of bathroom furniture that made its appearance in the years between 1800 and 1830: the bidet. This most controversial piece of bathroom equipment has attracted many high-flown and ridiculous names in its time: 'the hygienic little horse' in Italy, 'the hygienic guitar' in Spain, and in France ' the violin case' or* le petit indiscret. *Later in the century there were even double bidets – side by side or facing. It was the height of fashion to receive visitors while seated on the bidet, as indeed in the bath. Bathtubs at this period were oblong and made of tinned copper. Nude bathing had returned to favour and with it the licence to enjoy the sensation of lying in perfumed water. In this print by Pater (facing page) of circa 1730, the woman is alive with sensual anticipation as she steps into the bath, as the maid and her ladies in waiting busy themselves around her.*

The royal quarters apart, there must have been more than a hundred baths at Versailles, although those in the courtesans' wings, long since destroyed, would have been much less lavish. For in the middle years of the century, bathing was once again the pet preserve of the aristocracy. Writers picked up on the theme, as shown in the many descriptions that exist from this period; artists too rediscovered the harmonious curves of the naked female body in their paintings and prints. At court, it was in the best of taste to take baths, and to advertise the fact. It was perfectly usual to write letters in the bath, or even to entertain. Bathtubs were mostly portable, so one could enjoy a bath in any room you pleased.

Receiving visitors as you bathed was regarded as acceptable behaviour, as was the case with Marie-Antoinette's mentor the Abbé de Vermond, who gave audiences to bishops and ministers while in the bath. The same applies to the Duchesse de Châteauroux, who seemed to want to set the seal on her status as royal favourite by inviting Louis XV to attend her at her ablutions. He in turn invited a number of courtesans who were installed in an adjacent room, with the door left open so they could converse. After her bath, the Duchess 'retired to bed and dined there and everyone went back to her room', as the Maréchal de Richelieu tells us in his *Mémoires*. It is reminiscent of the communal baths in the Middle Ages, except for the differences in social status.

Madame de Genlis (1746–1830) was a notable woman of letters entrusted with the education of the children of the House of Orleans. In her *Mémoires*, she tells us: 'In Rome, in 1776, I used to bathe a lot, and as soon as I was in the bath, the Cardinal de Bernis would be alerted and he would come with his nephew to chat with me for three-quarters of an hour.' She continued this practice back in France and even went to Poitevin's public baths. At home in the château de Genlis, according to Gabrielle d'Estrées, she is said to have shared her large bathtub and famous baths of milk and rose petals with her sister-in-law. For baths taken in company, one could conceal one's nudity by adding some milk or bran to cloud the water, or there were baths available that had lids, either solid or made of cane, which also

*WHEREAS IN the seventeenth century it was 'woman at her toilette' that was the favourite subject for prints, in the eighteenth century it was 'woman in her bath', for bathing was again the new craze. It was the done thing to receive visitors and conduct flirtations in the bath. That did not of course prevent it from becoming the object of satire, as in **Monkey Business**, a painted panel by Christophe Huet (above), in which the bathers have the heads of chimpanzees. As for the 'bain de salon', there one would lightly veil one's nudity by the addition of a handful of bran or a pint of milk to the water. Evoking the sensuality of the eighteenth century, this scene of a woman emerging from a bath perfumed with hyssop vinegar (facing page) is in fact an advertisement for a manufacturer of luxury linens and was painted by Marchetti in 1906.*

served to keep in the heat. Madame du Châtelet, Voltaire's friend and inspiration, was not always careful to take these precautions. One day, as her valet Longchamp recalls in his *Mémoires*, the Marquise called him and asked him to take the kettle from beside the fire and top up her bath, which had not been clouded by the addition of milk. As she spread her legs, so as not to get burned, Longchamp averted his eyes and turned away. 'Careful, you'll burn me!' she cried. For a moment Longchamp was upset, and thought that great ladies regarded their servants just as part of the furniture.

The bath was like a sophisticated comedy of manners; to anyone sly enough it offered the chance of a glimpse of nudity with a perfectly calculated air of innocence. Casanova's *Mémoires* tell us that 'La Charpillon was in a big bathtub, head turned towards the door and the dreadful coquette, pretending

it was her aunt, did not move a muscle and addressed me: "Aunt, pass me the towels." She was in the most seductive posture and as the bath was only half full, I could enjoy all the attractions of a Venus-like body without the liquid which covered her like a light gauze in the least bit impeding my greedy gaze.'

The subtle sensuality and lazy pleasures of hot baths were bound to draw criticism. 'They have never been so widespread and so well known amongst us as latterly. Laziness and idleness have contributed greatly to establishing and maintaining them,' complained Madame de Genlis, a firm believer in the benefits of cold water. In reaction to the decadent reputation of hot baths, 'modern' or revolutionary spirits preached the virtues of cold baths, which underwent a minor revival towards the end of the eighteenth century. But whether hot or cold, the bath had again become a recognized part of life.

THIS SET photograph (above) of one of the opening scenes from Patrice Lecomte's film Ridicule *could well be seen to symbolize the revival in personal hygiene that occurred in the eighteenth century. After bathing, one would powder oneself all over with a light film that softened and smoothed the texture of the skin. Here two chambermaids are blowing powder from a porcelain dish so that it hangs in the air as a fine bluish cloud and clings to the body. Reminiscent of the same period (facing page) is the reproduction bathroom with a bath of tinned copper to retain the water's heat. In the foreground stands a fine Anjou-style chair-bidet. In the chair-back, under the padded headrest, the necessary toilet accessories are kept out of sight.*

BATHS, WASHSTANDS, 'PETITS INDISCRETS', WATER CANS AND WASH BASINS

After the eighteenth century, most people bathed in so-called 'modern' baths. These were no longer made of marble or of wood lined with lead, but of metal, usually tinned copper, the advantages of which were that it did not rust and kept the water hot. From 1770 onwards, there were also some models manufactured in metal that were easier to shape, such as tinplate, sometimes painted to look like enamel. The inside of the bathtub might be lined with tin, or even silver for luxury models. The outside was often covered in decorative painting. Some, built by cabinetmakers, were stylish pieces of furniture in their own right, caned or cushion-backed, in the shape of sofas, day-beds or chaises-longues for one or more persons. The end of the eighteenth century also saw the appearance of the famous 'boot', a type of slipper bath similar to that used by Marat and Benjamin Franklin. It was assembled from more than twenty pieces of metal, and was equipped with a funnel for filling it up and a tap for draining the contents away.

The *cabinets de bains* were often provided with two bathtubs, one for washing and one for rinsing. When these were fixed in position and plumbed in to tanks of water, they would be surmounted by a canopy to which muslin curtains were attached. If they were portable, they might be encased in wickerwork with a cover to keep the water hot and protect the bather's modesty, and could be transformed if desired into a stylish couch or armchair. These were the ancestors of what was known right up to the start of the twentieth century as the sitz-bath or hip-bath, which was in widespread use because it required less water. For precisely the same reason, there were many smaller baths for part-washing: foot-baths, arm-baths, and so on. As with the full-size bathtubs, more fanciful and elaborate versions existed of all these rather curious objects, made by cabinetmakers.

The second most important item of bathroom furniture was the washstand, on which stood a jug of water and a basin. In the eighteenth century, this was a proper piece of furniture, with drawers and compartments and a thousand and one clever touches and hidden contrivances; a speciality of French cabinetmakers, it was soon taken up by Chippendale, Hepplewhite and Sheraton in England. This elegant item of furniture was used principally for washing the face and hands. Gradually it evolved into the larger and more substantial washstand of the nineteenth century, with its marble top (an idea dating from the Empire period), which was suitable for use when washing the top half of the body.

It was in the eighteenth century that undoubtedly the most controversial of all these items was introduced, 'le petit indiscret' being only one of the many names given to the bidet. Although this equipment existed in the seventeenth century, it was first recorded in 1726, when Madame de Prie received the Marquis d'Argenson on her bidet. At a period when rooms for the intimate toilette were beginning to be introduced, and when morals were not so much lax as licentious, this aristocratic piece of furniture, often beautifully made, had not yet acquired its dubious reputation. It was used without distinction by men and women alike and was even the subject of engravings and paintings by masters such as Boucher and Watteau. Over the course of the century, the bidet was transformed into an elaborate piece of

FOR THE 'bain de salon', taken in company in the bedchamber, the cabinetmakers vied with one another in ingenuity and skill to produce baths that were pieces of furniture in their own right. These would be in the style of the period and would match the decor of any room in which they were placed. On this page of Boucher designs (facing page), the baths, either upholstered or faced with wickerwork, are disguised as bergère *easy chairs, in the case of the hip-bath or sitz-bath, and as couches, in the case of the full-length bathtub. Such models usually had lids to conceal the sheet-metal vessel, and these were often articulated to enable the bather to preserve his or her modesty, and also to keep the water hot. Doubtless the most efficient model in that respect was the 'boot' (above), a variant of the type of bath known in English as the slipper bath, the model used by Marat and Benjamin Franklin. Some had a heater to warm up the water; the fuel was spirits of wine, eventually replaced by coal, charcoal or methylated spirits.*

furniture, inspiring the most ingenious master-pieces of the cabinetmaker's art. In 1739, a Monsieur Perverie of the Rue aux Ours proposed a bidet in the shape of a violin, made of porcelain and supported, together with its carrying case, on a wooden base. There were also double bidets, arranged like love-seats, as well as models for officers on campaign, made of metal and with retractable legs, capable of 'resisting the fiercest shaking'. Madame de Pompadour's 'furnishings' were of a quite different sort. One was of rosewood inlaid with a floral decoration, the bowl of tin and the feet and ornaments of gilt bronze. The other was made of walnut, the bowl of Sèvres porcelain, the lid and back covered in red leather with gilded studs, with concealed compartments for two crystal bottles.

By the early nineteenth century, the bidet was reserved exclusively for female use. One of the last male users was probably Napoleon Bonaparte, who owned a number of bidets made by Biennais, one in silver gilt 'with a silver-gilt box for sponges and two bottles of diamond-cut crystal'. Women continued to use bidets, but now they concealed an object that was regarded as immodest. Stockists' catalogues included the bidet in their prices for a fully fitted bathroom, while the catalogues put out by the large stores offered a variety of models that could be delivered to the home. There is a true story about this – as 'true' as all true stories are – that a woman in the provinces was horrified to discover, when she checked the table arrangements for a dinner she was giving that evening, that her porcelain bidet occupied pride of place in the centre of the table. It had arrived that morning, and the butler had taken it to be 'Madame's new soup tureen'.

Although the bidet was adopted throughout southern Europe, it was never accepted in Britain (nor, later, in the United States), where it was always regarded as having a questionable reputation. One exception was the Duchess of Bedford, who apparently possessed a fine 'toilette' of French manufacture with a porcelain bidet tucked away inside; another was Sir Arthur Young who, in 1780, deplored the lack of this instrument for personal hygiene in England.

Bidets, portable baths, washstands, water cans and basins – all these new items necessary for keeping clean – were kept and used in the *garde-robe*, or wardrobe, that existed in most aristocrats' houses, not only in Paris but in the distant French provinces. At Le Puy, towards the turn of the century, we know the Bonnevilles possessed two washstands, with basin and water jug, one mirror and one hardwood bathtub.

At the same time, architects were beginning to install proper bathrooms in the mansions of aristocrats. Among them was Nicolas Le Camus de Mézières, who was a discriminating observer of the lifestyle of his contemporaries. In 1780 he identified the need for privacy and for spaces to which one could retreat in solitude, a need he believed was best met by the bathroom. 'Its decoration,' he added, 'should be carefully done so as to bring out the sensuality and refinement of the pleasures of the toilette.' Before the century was out, twenty out of sixty-six *hôtels particuliers* in Paris had bathrooms. All were exquisitely appointed.

At the Hôtel de Vergès in the Faubourg Saint-Honoré, the floor was a chequerboard of black and white tiles, the bath was set into an alcove decorated with frescoes, and its two copper taps were fed by three tanks of water overhead. The room was lit by natural light from a bay window glazed with Bohemian glass. The bathroom at the Hôtel de La Reynerie, Place Louis-XV, had a glass dome in imitation of that of the Pantheon, walls painted with white arabesques on a violet background in the Pompeian style, and a bath in an alcove draped with muslin, with a large mirror, made of a single sheet of glass hung at one end, as well as a boudoir, a *garde-robe* and an English-style water closet.

A magazine illustration of this time shows a

THE BIDET was made in the prevailing style of the day. This model (above) betrays Egyptian influences and, although it did not in fact belong to Napoleon, it would certainly have appealed to him. He was meticulous about personal hygiene and owned several bidets made by the best cabinetmakers and goldsmiths. It was an item used at first by both men and women, but by the mid-nineteenth century it came to be seen as exclusively feminine, and was therefore associated with loose morals. At a period when morality and fashion dictated that no part of the concealed and corseted body should be revealed, this lithograph by Maurin (facing page) – featuring two baths made of sheet metal – illustrates the perennial theme of nudity observed, and is subtitled 'Can he see anything?'.

'fully-equipped' bathroom: an upholstered chair/ bidet and, underneath a canopy with green silk hangings, a bathtub on a platform, its two taps in the shape of a lion's mouth. 'For,' the account concludes, 'rich people are beginning to have bathrooms ... not just for the summer but also for reasons of hygiene'. The taps were not, of course, connected to a water supply, but otherwise the illusion is perfect.

These baths installed 'in the houses of the great and good', to quote the *Encyclopédie*, consisted of 'a room with a bed to lie down on after emerging from the bath, a room containing the bathtub, a room with an outlet for water or *garde-robe, a cabinet de toilette,* a hot-air room to dry the linen and heat the water. These baths ought to have a small garden so that people who take such baths more because of indisposition than for cleanliness can take exercise without being seen.' Those who lacked the money to buy anything so luxurious could purchase a portable version, a complete bathroom that could be installed outside in a courtyard or garden. We know, for example, that in Paris in 1773, the Comtesse de

Béthune put up for sale: 'a transportable bathroom, comprising three pieces; the exteriors painted in a lattice pattern, with tank and lead pipe, two copper bathtubs, hangings, four-poster bed hung with Orange cloth, matching chairs and Brazilian rose-wood shelf.'

Reading these descriptions of fabulous bathrooms in Havard's *Dictionnaire de l'ameublement*, one realizes how many belonged to famous artistes, dancers or actresses, who traditionally would have been 'kept' women. For Mademoiselle Moisset of the Opéra Comique, there were engraved mirrors hanging between painted wooden panels, picked out in gold and wash 'in the Oriental style', with a bathtub in sculpted wood in the Renaissance style, lined with silvered copper. For Mademoiselle Devise, a dancer at the Opéra, there was a copper bath attractively upholstered in wickerwork, with its own hot-water cylinder. For Mademoiselle de La Panouse, there were wall-hangings with a pattern of swans and water plants. And finally, there were the three adjoining chintz-filled rooms that made up the most luxurious suite of bathrooms in the Ancien Régime, the property of that most distinguished of dancers, Mademoiselle Guimard, who lived in a mansion designed by Nicolas Ledoux.

This was one of the reasons why, in the nineteenth century, the practice of bathing was for so long held to be immoral. The nineteenth-century French novel made successful capital of the combination of voluptuous pleasure, femininity and wanton extravagance that was implied by these lavish surroundings: 'through a door that was almost always open, one could see the bathroom, all marble and mirrors, with the white shell of its bathtub, its silver pots and bowls, its crystal and ivory accessories...' wrote Zola in *Nana*.

IN THESE two paintings, the same soft warm light floods in through the window at the back of the room to reveal two very different scenes of women bathing. The contrast lies in the social class to which the subjects belong, for in La Toilette *(above) by L.M. Cochereau (1793–1817), there is no bathtub and the woman has about her all the time-honoured utensils for part-washing. The copper foot-bath in which she cleans her feet is in fact very little different from the model used by Marie-Antoinette at the Petit Trianon or Napoleon at the château of Fontainebleau. In contrast, the scarcely veiled nudity of the young woman painted in 1810 by J.B. Mallet in* The Gothic Bathroom *represents the theme of the aristocrat emerging from her bath. The painter was one of the best chroniclers of the interiors of his day. Here he shows a Neo-Gothic decor, which at the turn of the century was to be adopted by the British as the appropriate style of furnishing for the first bathrooms with running water.*

ENGLISH COMFORT

'Good God, whatever is that word? "comfortable"? ... Maybe it's a Russian word, I don't have to respond to that,' wrote Balzac in *La Vieille Fille*. Yet the origin of the word is in fact French, and before it was anglicized and took on its more familiar modern meaning, it used to mean 'comforting' in the sense of 'consoling'.

But the idea of comfort in bathrooms seems for a long time to have been foreign to France, where it was always confused with the luxuriousness – not in fact always very comfortable – of the vast *apparte-ments de bains*. What the word 'comfort' means for an English-speaker is something quite different from this taste for ostentation. It is more like the 'solid luxury' of Montesquieu's expression, a luxurious-

ness that is useful, rational, dedicated to personal well-being and stripped of gratuitous ostentation.

What the English meant by comfort, one might have begun to guess from the appearance in the mid-eighteenth century of an item of furniture that they regarded as merely functional. This was a type of washstand. The basin stood on a base about a metre (three feet) high, which was surmounted by a mirror and equipped with two shelves, one at the foot of the base for the water jug, the other just below the basin, for storing smaller items. It was this elegant piece of furniture that was to evolve into the cabinetmaker's highly sophisticated and practical fitted washstand, with an adjustable mirror that served also as a cover for the basin; compartments for soap, shaving or hairdressing accessories; and, in the case of larger models, large drawers that provided an ingenious storage solution for foot-baths, hip-baths, etc.

THE BRITISH, with their taste for comfort, were the first to perfect the bathroom with hot and cold running water. However, the fine Gothic bathroom that would have graced the larger houses would have been for the use of members of the family only. Outsiders such as the governess would have had to manage with a hip-bath. In this delightful watercolour by Alice Squire (1840–1936) of The Governess, *a hip-bath appears in the foreground. Such an item might be made of sheet metal or tinned copper, and would be filled each day with pails of hot water brought up by the chambermaid. Also visible is a washstand with towels, and the usual porcelain ewer and basin for washing the hands and face.*

Even before the invention and installation of the famous British plumbing, these items of furniture quite transformed the experience of washing, making it a pleasurable event. The philosopher and historian Taine was amazed when he went to England during the 1860s: 'In my room ... two washstands, each with two drawers, the first equipped with an adjustable mirror, the second furnished with a large and small pitcher and a medium-sized one for hot water, two porcelain basins, a brush-holder, two soap dishes, a carafe with glass, a bowl with glass. Below that, a third very low washing-stand, a bucket, another bowl, a large, flat zinc bath for morning ablutions. In a cabinet, a towel rack with four different sorts of towels, one thick and springy.... The maid comes to the room four times a day: in the morning to ... bring a large jug of hot water with a woollen towel to put your feet on; at midday and seven in the evening to bring water and so forth, so the guest can wash before lunch and dinner; at night to close the windows, make the bed ready, set out the bath and change the linen.... The Englishman's expenditure on service and comfort is vast, and it has been said in jest that he spends a fifth of his life in his bath.'

This concern for comfort was all part of the wider British love of home life, and also their different understanding of hygiene and bodily cleanliness, for they had no bourgeois or religious reservations about water, and their attitudes towards cleanliness were punctilious to say the least. So it was during the nineteenth century, even before running water was widely available, that the British perfected a concept of the bathroom, the quality and diversity of which were

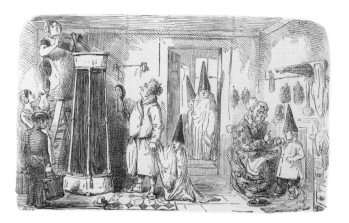

unrivalled. It was a style of comfort that corresponded to a particular lifestyle, a particular taste for domesticity. Once there was a supply of water and the gas to heat it, and given the talents of British engineers and plumbers, it was not long before the atmosphere of domestic intimacy could be fully recreated in surroundings where absolutely everything one needed was to hand: water running hot from the taps of bath and washbasin, the room heated and the bath towels warm as one emerged from the bath or shower. In such a cosy place as this, how could one not, in the original sense of the word, feel oneself 'comforted'?

France did not remain impervious to the notion of English comfort, seeing it as a perfectly useful, sensible and functional variant on French luxury, focused on the well-being of the person, 'born of the technical civilization and advancing in step with it', as P. Perrot wrote in *Le luxe*. But the French were slow to be convinced. It was not until the lifting of religious and bourgeois prohibitions on bathing and nudity, coupled with the widespread availability of running water, that the English model prevailed. In the meantime, princes and bourgeoisie alike indulged in the delights of the bath and the toilette in rooms that were more like salons than bathrooms.

In the First Empire period, when Napoleon used to take a steaming hot bath every day, the salon was very much the inspiration for the ravishing bathrooms at Malmaison and Rambouillet, while the

THE SUBJECT of this print (above, top) by John Leech is not, as it may seem, a Hallowe'en fancy dress party. What it actually shows is an English family around 1850 preparing to take a shower. As showerbaths were a recent invention, people feared the flow of water directly onto the head might cause fractures or even brain damage. The curious headgear was an acceptable alternative, especially when one hears the tale Montaigne tells about his visit to bathrooms in Italy: 'As for the custom they practise there of having the top of their heads shaved and putting on the bald patch a small piece of fabric or woollen cloth tied in place with fillets or bandages, my smooth head needed nothing done to it at all!' This English model of a shower (above) did not require running water as there was a reservoir that could be filled by hand. There was also a more advanced system with a hand pump.

bathroom at Fontainebleau had a most original bath, being clad with a mahogany panel like a chest of drawers, with false drawers and handles in bronze gilt. In Empress Marie-Louise's boudoir, the bath was hidden beneath a small platform, on which a couch was placed in the afternoons. The accommodation at the Élysée Palace was rather more lavish, consisting of a large room kept warm by means of a vast, white marble fireplace and an enormous carpet, with the painted mirrors on the walls providing reflections of the superb chandelier.

The most astonishing Empire period bathroom was without doubt that in the Hôtel de Beauharnais, restored in the 1960s and now the private residence of the German ambassador to Paris. Decorated in 1804, for Eugène de Beauharnais, son of Josephine, it caused Napoleon to go into a blind rage over its cost! Reminiscent of the East, with its blend of elaboration and restraint, this small gem (illustrated below), although occupying a space of no more than sixteen

square metres (one hundred and sixty square feet), seems as big as the mosque at Cordoba. This is due to the slender marble columns set around the bath and against the four walls, the mirrored surfaces of which reflect and multiply them to infinity. To one side is a small salon, more directly Turkish in inspiration. In shades of blue and gold, it echoes the layout of the bathroom, with a sofa in place of the bath and small columns surmounted by coupled arches.

PORTABLE BATHS AND BATHS DELIVERED TO THE HOME

The fact remains that these sophisticated installations bore absolutely no relation at all to the bathing habits of the majority of the population. Bathrooms were extremely rare, and the bath itself, usually portable, would be placed in one of the living rooms. At bathtime it could be moved to wherever there was space, usually in the hall. Stéphane Mallarmé tells the story that he was at the home of Nina de Callias, and saw Édouard Manet neatly folding up his overcoat and putting it down on what in the semi-darkness of the entrance-way he had taken to be the iridescent surface of a marble slab, but which was in fact the surface of the bathwater. The poet records that he stood by helplessly as he watched the sad death by drowning of the great man's coat. The

THE SECOND half of the eighteenth century saw a move towards suites of smaller bathrooms in many of the châteaux and large mansions, using for this purpose the private area known as the garde-robe, or wardrobe, the rooms of which served to accommodate all the objects needed for personal hygiene, including the chaise percée or commode. After the Revolution, the new order of 'nobility' lavished care and attention on their decor, and in this way maintained the traditions of the grand siècle. An antique style of decor (facing page) features in Napoleon's bathroom of 1807 in the Château de Rambouillet, with the bathtub set into an alcove and painted ceilings and panels representing the achievements of the Empire. His adoptive son's bathroom at the Hôtel de Beauharnais, restored at vast expense by the Empress Eugénie (above, left), was to provoke one of the Emperor's legendary outbursts of temper. When he read the totals of the bills to be settled he simply confiscated the whole mansion. All the bathtubs at Schloss Glienicke in Berlin were based on this Roman-inspired bath (above, right) designed by Karl Friedrich Schinkel (1781–1841).

practice of placing the bath in the hall was sufficiently well established for it to be used in a play by Feydeau, that fine observer of the manners of his day. In *Un bain de ménage*, a husband returns home and cries out in astonishment at his discovery of a bath in the antechamber. The response he receives has more than a hint of reproach: 'Where else am I supposed to have a bath, we haven't got a bathroom?'

The unusual location may perhaps be explained by the simple proximity of the front door, where the bathwater was delivered; at the dawn of the nineteenth century, little had been achieved in the way of bringing piped water into private homes. To fill the bathtub, one would have to send servants to the river Seine or to the fountain, or one could engage the services of the itinerant porters who delivered filtered drinking water in buckets or barrels, although its sale was strictly controlled. After carrying the pails of water to the correct floor of the apartment house, it still had to be heated and transferred to the bath. Afterwards, the water had to be emptied away, and that, given the absence of mains drainage, meant repeating the procedure in reverse, unless one had the effrontery simply to open the window instead. Some privileged people enjoyed at

least the illusion of running water, although the taps were actually connected to a tank that had to be refilled at regular intervals. As for methods of obtaining hot water, everyone had to fend for themselves. In the later years of the century, when someone wanted a bath at the home of the Marquis de Bonneval 'you gave two hours' notice to the valet whose duty it was to light the wood-burning stove, which was equipped with a pipe, the mouth of which dipped in the bath; the water arrived hot in the zinc vessel, which was painted on the outside to

IN PARIS, even as late as the 1870s, running water was rarely available except in the homes and apartments of the super-rich. The rest either had to pretend – by concealing tanks of water behind partitions – or simply have their servants fill the bathtubs with cans of water. That may well be the situation in this print of Romantic inspiration Emerging from the Bath *(facing page), after a drawing by Devéria (1800–57), where the act of taking a bath requires the presence of the chambermaid. With a guaranteed supply of hot water, there was no need for anyone else to be present, as we may observe in this work (above) by the Belgian society painter Alfred Stevens (1823–1906). The woman can drift into a peaceful reverie in her copper bath, a flower in one hand, without having to bother that the water is getting cold and to summon the maid. And even if you were not one of the lucky ones, you could still order a bath to be delivered to your home, conveyed to you by a specialist firm of the type seen in the print (above, top), who not only supplied the bath and its contents but emptied it as well.*

resemble marble' (a reminder of the marble baths of aristocratic châteaux).

Baths delivered to your door provided a neat solution to the problem. 'At a trot, the liquid rig arrives at your door, with bath, robe and sheet, everything is brought to you, even on the top floor': such was the service offered by Les Thermophores of 10, Rue du Faubourg-Montmartre. A bath could be ordered day or night and, according to the bather's preference, it could be hot, cold or even of mineral water. Originally a German idea, the service was launched in France in 1819 by a Monsieur Villette. It was an immediate success. It allowed Parisians – and above all Parisiennes – to observe hygiene and enjoy the pleasures of the bath without going to establishments in the town; no woman who cared for her reputation wanted to undress in a public place. If one could bathe at home, the problem was resolved. Horse-drawn vehicles would arrive with tanks full of hot water. The barrel-like reservoirs had a double lining, with the space between the walls filled with air. In order to fit the bathtub into tiny lift cages, some firms had devised leather baths that could be folded, or even retractable metal baths. Once at the correct floor, the bath was installed in the apartment and filled with buckets of water. Afterwards, the simplest method of drainage was by means of a hose running all the way down the stairs and into the gutter.

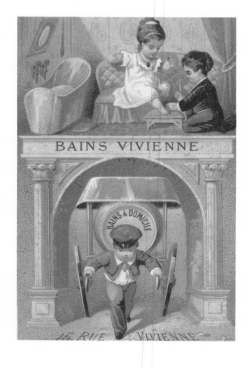

Home bathing was the subject of many comic stories and songs; it even provided the title for Paul de Kock's play *Les Bains à domicile*, performed at the Palais-Royal in 1845. It mentions a trick apparently common at that time: when a friend was having a dinner party, one would order several baths to be delivered at his house, all at the same time.

In the tradition of the English dandies who spent several hours getting ready to go out, Barbey d'Aurevilly used to have a bath sent up to him every morning from the famous Bains Chinois on the Boulevard des Italiens. Yet, although baths of this type were much discussed and written about, we know that, in 1838, the grand total of baths delivered to the home was just 1,013.

But there were hints already of the huge upheavals to come in the second half of the nineteenth century. By resulting in the rapid growth of the towns, the Industrial Revolution forced town planners to embark on major works to shore up the infrastructure and improve sanitation. In Paris, between 1860 and 1870, piped water was at last made available to the apartment houses, first on the Right Bank, and then on the Left. The first drinking fountains appeared in the streets. In the privately owned mansions around the Faubourg Saint-Honoré and the Rue du Roule, it was now possible for the *cabinets de bains* to be moved up one storey. On the Champs-Élysées, one can still visit the extravagant bathroom of La Païva, a high-class prostitute of the period, who possessed a half-sunken bath, plated on the inside with silver with copper inlay, the taps set with cabochon turquoises and the exterior clad in onyx, as too were the lower parts of the walls, the fireplace and the basins. The decor was in the Moorish style (as was the marquetry of the portable bidet), the mirrors were set into horseshoe arches, there were ceramics on a turquoise ground, and running all the way round the ceiling was a cornice made up of little stalactites of crystal. Bathrooms rather less lavish than this one began to feature in the plans for the bourgeois apartment blocks then under construction,

BATHS BROUGHT to the door were the ideal solution for those without running water. There were some high-class public bathing establishments, such as the Bains Vivienne (above), that offered a delivery service with or without bathtub, inclusive of the finest and whitest linen. For the majority of the population, however, the chore of fetching water was far from over; going to collect water from the public fountain, storing it and heating it was the harsh reality of daily life, as illustrated (facing page) by Bonvin. In an effort to make life simpler, a man called Robin devised around 1880 an automatic distributor operating from public fountains. It supplied water heated to between 65° C (149° F) and 90° C (194° F) at a rate of eight litres (fourteen pints) of water for five centimes. Although it caused a sensation, the system suffered from lack of maintenance, as well as unexpected explosions.

IN THE nineteenth century, in palaces and opulent dwellings all over the world, elaborately decorated and furnished bathrooms tended to be either Neo-classical or Oriental in their inspiration. The bathroom (above) of the Empress Maria Alexandrovna in the Winter Palace at St Petersburg was Roman in style. The bathtub is set into an apse with a semicircular vaulted dome in the Pompeian manner. In the same palace, there is a Turkish extravaganza by Bryullov, the favourite decorator of the Empress Alexandra Feodorovna, its over-elaborate decoration (facing page) tending to overwhelm the intricate stonework, horseshoe arches and slender columns. The height of the room means that it is unlikely that the minimum temperature of the room was 25° C (77° F), which is said to have been maintained.

while existing residents tried to find some odd corner to squeeze one in.

It was at this period that scientific and medical discoveries demonstrated the imperative need for hygienic measures to be introduced throughout the population. The second half of the nineteenth century seized on hygiene as a credo of popular education. A clean body was the key to social order, virtue and morality. To win over the bourgeoisie and evangelize the rest, a spate of handbooks was published on subjects such as 'looking after your body' and 'how to keep your apartment clean'. By the end of the century, these had acquired the grandiose title of 'treatises on hygiene'. All rehabilitated the bath and hot, or at least warm, water, and for the first time in the history of baths and bathing, the magic word 'soap' was heard.

Baths continued to have an aura of sensuality and licentiousness attaching to them (as we have seen, apart from the very wealthy, it was the kept actresses, the prostitutes and the brothels who had bathrooms), and this disturbed women customers. To persuade 'gentlewomen' of the innocence of the practice, it was necessary to demonstrate that the bath offended against neither religion, modesty nor morality, but constituted on the contrary one of the great virtues of the bourgeois class. The Comtesse de Bassanville emphasized this point in 1859: 'A woman who is clean and tidy is almost always virtuous and a gentlewoman. Washing is to the body what education is to the mind.' By the turn of the century, the message had been understood: cleanliness was a necessity, and washing was not necessarily immoral.

Only then was it possible for the notion of 'learning to take care of your body' to be accompanied by some sense of self-regard, or even pleasure.

THE *CABINET DE TOILETTE*: TEMPLE OF FEMININITY

'You can deceive a woman, but you should never take her by surprise', said Sébastien Mercier in his *Tableaux de Paris*. That was precisely the philosophy adopted by the nineteenth-century bourgeoisie in respect of the *cabinet de toilette*.

Where the very rich had a bathroom, the well-to-do occupants of the apartments on the boulevards had a *cabinet de toilette* adjacent to the master bedroom, in the private quarters. It was installed in a sort of alcove, usually windowless, and concealed by no more than a curtain so as to let the air circulate. The equipment was basic: basin and water pot on a washstand, sometimes a bidet and a large bucket for waste water. As there was no running water, if there was a bath it would be portable.

For many years it remained a private place reserved for the most intimate ablutions, a sort of temple to female beauty. At the turn of the century, the Baronne de Staffe, the Comtesse de Bassanville, the Comtesse d'Alq, the Marquise de Garches, the Comtesse de Tramar, the Marquise de Pompeillan and the Comtesse de Gencé all wrote down their ideas of what the *cabinet de toilette* of a 'gentlewoman' should be like.

'The *cabinet de toilette* must be a completely private place,' declared the Comtesse de Tramar. 'It is a woman's sanctuary, the holy of holies,' insisted the Baronne de Staffe. It was a place for concealing 'the indiscreet items which reveal too personal an aspect of life,' advised the Marquise de Pompeillan. Bathtubs, bidets and other baths, as well as the whole battery of water jugs, buckets and bowls, a little too reminiscent of personal hygiene,

IN THE large mansions of late-nineteenth century Paris, the moneyed bourgeoisie spent fortunes on bathrooms – although the women who bathed in them were not always wives, as Balzac makes clear in Splendeurs et Misères des courtesans *when he describes Esther's toilette. 'She bathed and then proceeded to this minutely detailed toilette unfamiliar to the majority of women in Paris, for it takes too long and is hardly undertaken by anyone except courtesans or grand ladies who have all the day to call their own.' A fine example is the Moorish bathroom of La Païva (facing page and above, showing the detail of a medallion), who was a high-class prostitute in the latter years of the century. The walls are clad in onyx, as too is the bathtub, which has a silver lining bearing an inlaid frieze in worked copper. Onyx has the very considerable advantage over marble in that it is warm to the touch, but it is susceptible to variations in temperature, which is why the bath is metal-lined. Today, in the palaces of Arab emirs, the bottom of the bathtub is heated and maintained at a constant temperature to prevent it from cracking.*

should be banished from sight after use with the wave of a magic wand, leaving the beauties of the place itself to gratify the eye. Concern for cleanliness being associated with the principle of femininity, the *cabinet de toilette* was principally Madame's preserve. If Monsieur was not lucky enough to have his own and used his wife's, it should never be in her presence, and then only on condition of being quick and putting away his shaving kit and toilet items so as to remove all trace of his presence.

Although the *cabinet de toilette* was strictly private, great care had to be taken over its decoration and layout. 'For women of quality, the *cabinet de toilette* should be stylish rather than comfortable,' the Baronne de Staffe advised. To which Madame de Gencé added: 'During the hours of the toilette we must not find ourselves overcome with boredom.'

These are prescriptions for an ideal place, a room billowing with fine materials, flounces, hangings and curtains of chintz, muslin, tulle and cretonne. Charming, but hardly hygienic. Not that that mattered very much, for once the washing was done and the immodest utensils cleared away, it became a place devoted to beauty and the care of the appearance. There would be one or two frosted glass windows masked with curtains, a chandelier on the ceiling and a pastel-coloured carpet on the floor.

As for the furniture, it would comprise two washstands of the same shape, one opposite the other. The larger would be reserved for minor ablutions and equipped with a ewer and basin made of porcelain or silver, along with accessories such as a soap dish. Above it would be a shelf for perfume bottles, lotions and vinegars. The smaller model, equipped with a large, adjustable mirror framed in a satin and lace frill, would be reserved for dressing the hair. In addition there would be two armchairs, one on either side, a cheval-glass and a variety of pouffes, gilded folding chairs and stools, together with a chaise-longue or sofa on which to rest after bathing. One would be almost unaware of the equipment stored behind the cretonne frills, in cupboards or in another room: the bidet, the bath and the tub – the last item the usual choice to be brought out for the daily sponge bath.

That form of washing (known in France as 'the English wash') was the ancestor of the shower. Traditionally, cold water would have been used for its invigorating qualities, but when hot water was employed, the tub represented a serious gesture towards cleanliness. It was a round vessel made of zinc, enamel or even silver, and was shallow, portable and equipped with a funnel-shaped spout for filling and drainage. The British were intrepid travellers, accustomed to bracing themselves for the discomforts of the continent and more distant parts, so they also invented a travelling bath, a large metal basin that served both as tub and hip-bath, equipped with a lid with catch and straps and, sometimes, retractable feet. Later, the travel tub would be made of rubber. There were even smaller lightweight models of paper mâché as a cheap alternative, which

IN THE second half of the nineteenth century, the cabinet de toilette *was the temple of femininity, a place of frills and furbelows, a sort of salon dedicated to minor ablutions and beauty care, from which the masculine presence was banned. As the splendid room (facing page, top) used by the Empress Eugénie at the Château de Saint-Cloud would suggest (recorded here in a watercolour by Fortuné de Fournier), the* cabinet de toilette *generally had at least one window, a washstand with matching ewer and basin in decorated porcelain, a dressing-table, a cheval-glass, an easy chair, two upright chairs and a small table for taking tea in company. Plainer and more practical (above) is the pine washstand with articulated mirror so attractively painted by Mary Cassatt in 1891; entitled* La Toilette, *the picture shows a woman washing the top half of her body in a bowl of hot water. An English style of Art Nouveau (facing page, bottom) characterizes these extraordinary items pictured in* The Cabinet Maker *of August 1897, which illustrate ingenious methods of camouflaging baths and washbasins.*

could be reused until they began to let in water. But one had to be alert to signs of a possible split.

It took no more than a couple of minutes to have a wash in the tub, preferably in the morning. The correct English method was to put in the cold water and sponge before entering the tub, which is why there were some advanced models that thoughtfully provided an arrangement for keeping one's feet dry when stepping in! You would start by washing the back of the neck, then the head, the chest and so on down to the feet, ending with the arms. You then got dry by rubbing yourself down with a horsehair glove

or rough towel, so as not to get cold. You could also add to the final rinse a glass of eau de Cologne or even whisky, and finish up with some sort of warming exercise.

In the course of his reminiscences, Prince Poniatowski recalled his own experience of the tub: 'In the mornings, in each bedroom on a square of waxed cloth, a sponge in ten centimetres of cold water reposed in the centre of a large tub in enamelled zinc; within reach of the hand was the soap, a can of hot water for chilly mortals, and as you got out, a horsehair glove on a litre of eau de Cologne, and finally a bathrobe and towels: this was the system of washing favoured by the most particular people.' The Comtesse de Tramar may have regarded the fashionable practice of 'tubbing' as a sort of snobbery but the Comtesse de Gencé heartily recommended it, if one had no full-size bathtub. It was in fact the most common method of washing, and the *cabinet de toilette* and its equipment became almost a cliché of the paintings of the time.

As for the bathroom proper, which was still something of a rarity in France, it would be decorated in much the same style as the *cabinet de toilette*. Even on the threshold of the twentieth century, the French were still caught up in an old-fashioned notion of a place whose cleansing function had to be obscured at all costs in favour of its role as a temple of beauty. There was no trace of English comfort and convenience in the bathroom described by Émile Zola in his *Carnets*, which he used as the model for that of Renée Saccard. The drapery against the walls has 'a pink muslin ground, folded into wide pleats, each pleat separated by a large ornament of appliquéd guipure. This drapery hangs down like a tent from the ceiling, where it is held in place by a silver dome. There are silver fillets running down to each guipure ornament.... On the floor, a carpet of white and grey moquette and a large black bear-skin. In a corner facing the windows, the muslin tent opens to reveal a pink marble bathtub, and above it a Venetian mirror in a silver frame.... The bath is the shape of a shell; two silver taps pour water into it; you enter the bath down marble steps. Inlaid silver table for the toilet utensils, in ivory marked with her

AT THE end of the nineteenth century, the tub was the most usual way of taking a bath. In Claudine in Paris, *Colette dismissed it as English snobbery: '... and no tub, no. Instead of the tub, which freezes your feet, ridiculous with its noisy theatrical thunderclaps, a wooden bucket, a vat, that's it! A good wooden vat of Montigny wood, hooped beech, in which I can sit cross-legged in the hot water, and which scrapes the behind in an agreeable fashion.' We should at least thank the sponge-bath for inspiring painters to produce so many superb nudes depicted taking their daily bath. Among them was Anders Zorn, the major Swedish exponent of Impressionism, who in his watercolour of 1888 entitled* The Tub *(above) wonderfully conveys that exquisite gesture of the sponge squeezed against the breasts. In this fine pastel of 1883 (facing page), Degas shows* The Woman in Her Tub *gently wiping the underside of her arm.*

*Tub, BATHTUB, bidet, foot-bath, bowls and water can (above) are all those items made of sheet metal
and zinc 'which reveal too personal an aspect of life' according to the Marquise de Pompeillan in*
Le Guide de la femme du monde, *and which should therefore be carefully concealed after use. For at the end
of the nineteenth century, modesty was offended by 'any glance directed at an appliance whose relations with
your person are too intimate not to be kept secret,' adds the Comtesse de Tramar in* La Bréviaire de la femme.
*Today, such bathing accessories in good condition and with an attractive patina are much sought after for bathing
in the garden. Before he even picked up his brushes, Bonnard took wonderful preparatory photographs for his
paintings, among them many of his wife Marthe, who loved bathing. This superb photograph taken against
the light is called* Marthe in the Tub *(facing page).*

nically and in its inspiration, placing the accent on hygiene and ease of use rather than on any aesthetic considerations – their first reaction was one of total incomprehension and outright rejection: 'a laboratory', 'factories to get washed in' were among the first comments heard.

But gradually the designated washing place shed its feminine trappings. Enclosed within smooth pastel walls that did not collect dirt, dust or germs, the appliances, now fixed in place and supplied with running water, were designed to be functional and to fulfil precise roles. The new bathroom gradually replaced the *cabinet de toilette*, and in so doing set the seal on the union of cleanliness and beauty.

At first, bathrooms tended to be installed next to the kitchen, because that was the only source of water, and the *cabinet de toilette* therefore continued in use for matters of personal hygiene until such time as both activities could be reunited in a room next to the bedroom. Before that could happen, there were many problems that had to be resolved: the internal layout of apartments needed to be re-planned, methods of insulating internal pipes and making them watertight had to be found, a hot water supply had to be installed and mass-produced products had to be designed. Only when all this had been achieved was it possible for the separate bathroom adjacent to the bedroom to become the norm, adapted to fit all kinds of home.

monogram in silver. *Toilette* of pink marble, cupboard with double-panelled mirror inlaid with silver. One chaise-longue, two pouffes.'

This was exactly the sort of decor that Madame de Staffe dreamed of, that 'of those select few rich women, artists and so forth, the walls clad in onyx and marble panels, the windows with Oriental hangings, and the ceiling with lanterns of iridescent pink crystal'. The pink marble bath was to be in the shape of a shell. Beside it, 'a carpet made of pieces of cut-out leather joined together'. Behind a silken curtain, 'the shower apparatus, with a soft rain or violent jet for the satin skin of the divinity of the place'. She further specified that all the appliances be supplied with taps for hot, cold and warm water, and that the tub be made of porcelain decorated with arum lilies, water lilies and nenuphars.

When visitors to the Exhibition of Hygiene held in Paris in 1900 first saw the American bathroom – an entirely revolutionary concept both tech-

If France finally managed to make the leap from the frilled and furbelowed *cabinet de toilette* to the en suite bathroom of today, it was by making a small detour via Britain, where the genius of British plumbing first invented a modern bathroom of a comfort and convenience unsurpassed for more than half a century.

THE ENGLISH tradition, illustrated in this drawing of 1909 (above) by L. Sabatier, was to spend two minutes in a tub of cold water every morning. Prince Poniatowski recalls in his Souvenirs de jeunesse *how he remained faithful to the tub for fifteen years, believing that a young man, whether emerging from his bed or after vigorous exercise (marching, horseriding, boxing or fencing), 'finds in a tub of cold water a tonic he cannot expect of the debilitating action of a bath in warm water'. For bathing a child, however, as in this coloured print by E. Defonte of 1896 (above, top), doctors recommend that the water be kept at about 36° C (97° F). The bath provides the pretext for endless fun, even for the sons of a king. When Louis XIII was a child he got into his bath at seven o'clock and stayed there until a quarter to eight. It was not until around 1860 that people enjoyed the convenience of having hot water ready and waiting in a gleaming copper boiler. That delight lies in store for this young woman still heavy with sleep as she prepares in the morning light for* Bathtime, *interpreted here by the Spanish painter Ramón Casas (facing page).*

THE MODERN
BATHROOM

O TRACE the history of the modern bathroom, with all the comfort and convenience it
represents, we need to follow a path that
starts in England and leads finally to the United
States. The desire for comfort in bathrooms did not
really begin to impinge until the 1830s. When the
decade began, even Buckingham Palace still had no
proper bathroom. It was in 1837, the year of Queen
Victoria's coronation, that Parliament examined a
scheme to bring hot water to Her Majesty's bedroom. And yet only thirty or so years later, at Bear
Wood in Berkshire, bathrooms with running water
were included in the original building plans.

THE ENGLISH BATHROOM

The two essential elements of the famous English
bathroom were a vast washstand and – once it was
connected to the water supply – a double-walled
porcelain bath, custom-made, and boxed in with
mahogany. Because of the quality of craftsmanship
of these two elements, from 1850 to 1910 the English bathroom was without rival. That is why they
were installed by the jet set all over the world, by
princes in St Petersburg, Indian rajahs, American
millionaires and, on Fifth Avenue, by the architect
George Vanderbilt, the pioneer of the modern high-
tech bathroom.

The English wash hand-stand developed out of the
smaller rectangular washstand with a marble or
ceramic tile top, drawers and a shelf at the bottom to
stand water cans, buckets and foot-baths. It would
have been situated in the dressing room, or in the
bedroom, and if it was a double room there would
have been two of them. It was subsequently transformed into a full-scale piece of furniture, more like
a chest-of-drawers, with an upper section housing a
small reservoir of water, used to supply the porcelain
or brass bowl set into a marble slab. A little later, the

*'ARE YOU a bath person or a shower person? It is impossible to exaggerate the character-revealing difference
between the two,' wrote Michel Tournier in* Le Miroir des idées. *The contrasting pleasures of shower and
bath are illustrated here by the calm contentment of Bibi in her bath, on honeymoon with photographer
Jacques-Henri Lartigue in 1920 (page 118), and the joyful vivacity of the heroine of the German film*
Brand in der Oper *of 1930 (page 119). Bathroom furnishings evolved over a long period, starting from the point
where the wooden cabinet became more important than the functional washstand it enclosed, thus
elevating a functional object into an art object. In this 'medieval' masterpiece of a washstand (facing page),
the soap dishes are hidden in the tops of the towers. Only with Art Nouveau did what Maurice Rheims calls*
art sanitaire *truly begin, as exemplified by this Chelsea bathroom (above) that is oddly reminiscent of
an interior by Van de Velde.*

basin was suspended on a tilting mechanism so the water could be tipped away into a large vessel for waste liquid. It was Hellyer, the Prince of Wales' ingenious plumber, who designed a waste outlet with a down-pipe to replace this rather insalubrious arrangement.

Connected to the water supply soon after 1870, the wash hand-stand developed into an imposing item of bathroom furniture, sometimes with one basin, sometimes two, and sometimes also a small shower attachment for washing the hair and the then fashionable beard. The plumbing was concealed behind mahogany carvings and the central panel stopped just short of the floor, leaving a space to place one's feet and stand in comfort. Behind the doors on either side were a portable foot-bath and hip-bath (on the continent it would have been a

bidet) which slid out on stands. Everything was designed to be within hand's reach; there were rails on either side to hang towels; below the mirror were fitted dishes for soap and sponge, and a holder for the mug. Originally manufactured only in England, this expensive, high-quality model was soon to be imitated and reproduced by all the big foreign manufacturers. Once situated in the bedchamber or dressing-room, it reverted to the bathroom when the bath was plumbed in.

To accompany this magnificent item, the English invented the large, double-walled porcelain bathtub. Moulded in one piece and hand-crafted, it was wider, longer and higher than previous models (gone was the obsession with not wasting hot water or letting it get cold, thanks to the invention in 1868 of the geyser, the first proper gas-fuelled water heater).

THIS MONUMENTAL bath-cum-shower (facing page) represents the state of the art in late-nineteenth-century English bathrooms. Installed in a London home in 1895, it is encased in mahogany, and features copper taps, an overhead shower, side jets and a whirlpool bath. The washstand is built in the same style – it cannot be seen here because at this date it occupied a separate wall. During the first decade of the twentieth century, not only did bathroom layouts change, the individual elements also reflected a new willingness to accept sanitary ware that did not seek to disguise its function. The sublime London bathroom of 1904 (above) is typical of the new look, with its huge porcelain bath with boule feet, washbasin on a cabled pedestal and shower consisting of a nickel-plated frame above a base. Curtains and rugs have been replaced by tiled mosaics. Only the chandelier looks to the past. As a mark of changing times, there is now space for exercising, as well as a massage table.

Porcelain was the heaviest of materials (baths could weigh more than five hundred kilos (one thousand pounds) and it was also the most expensive. As well as being a means of showing off one's wealth, since models made of zinc, copper or enamelled metal were much more reasonably priced, it also offered an impeccable white surface, long, if not everlasting, life and ease of maintenance – and it felt good to the touch. To match the elaborate washstands, baths were boxed in behind mahogany panels and abutted against carved frames inlaid with decorative ceramics, designed to protect the walls against splashes.

No doubt the ultimate degree of luxury and ostentation was achieved by the bath with built-in 'sentry-box' shower, which, with its solid carved panels and cabled columns, has all the trappings of pseudo-Gothic grandeur. This monumental item consists of a bathtub capable of providing a whirlpool bath and a boxed-in shower cabinet. The large, centrally mounted showerhead provides the traditional downwardly directed spray, while from the three sides horizontal and vertical jets of water are released at varying pressures through many small holes in the inner wall. These jets are controlled by an impressive array of gleaming copper taps that run in a line down the outside. Queen Victoria had a bath like this at Osborne House on the Isle of Wight – apparently the taps were so big they resembled the controls of a boiler on a warship.

Up to around 1880, even large houses would have had only one bathroom for family use. Guests would have made do with the euphemistically entitled hip-bath provided in the bedrooms. Some of the old aristocracy considered modern bathrooms irredeemably vulgar and stayed faithful to the tub, and some houses such as Carlton Towers in Humberside, although built after 1870, had no bathroom at all.

The decor of the English bathroom at this period was almost oppressively magnificent. Although there were generally one or two windows in the room, the light was filtered through panes of coloured glass bearing designs of birds, plants and flowers, and the curtains were weighty affairs laden with tassels and braid. Walls and floor were covered in ceramic tiles, with rugs to keep the feet warm. The area provided enough space to exercise. The bath and washbasins occupied different walls, while the hip-baths and foot-baths and even accessories

IN THE late nineteenth century, the English attempted to produce less expensive bathroom furniture by searching for an alternative to mahogany panels. An obvious area for experimentation was cast iron, a material already used for bridges and the hulls of ships. The first cast-iron washstands appeared in catalogues (above, top) with basin and surround made of marble or porcelain, and integral mirrors and shelves. Then came the first bathtubs. Unsurpassed by any other material, cast-iron became the most popular choice for baths, among them the famous model standing on lion's paw feet (above, left, shown with shower), which remains a bestseller even today. This particular example, which has English taps, is installed in the Hotel Hidiv Kasri in Istanbul on the Bosphorus, formerly the palace of the Viceroy of Egypt. For the hundred or more years that its traditions of service have attracted celebrities from all over the world, the Savoy Hotel in London (facing page) has retained the original decor of its bathrooms. The washbasin is set into a marble fitment supported on nickel-plated legs, and a large shower rose still sits above the porcelain bath.

such as the brass towel-rails and washing equipment were all tidied away behind mahogany panels. In comparison with its French counterpart, it represented a radically different approach to bathroom decor, being altogether more austere and less specifically feminine.

True, the English bathroom was not yet the private space it would eventually become. It was a furnished room, and as such was treated almost like any other; it was not situated next to the master bedroom but was used by all the members of the family. In this form, in more or less luxurious versions, it was adopted by the affluent middle classes throughout Europe. Bathroom decor did not really begin to change until the end of the century, and when it did so it was largely because of the availability of a new material, cast iron.

If the English were pioneers in plumbing, water supply and mains drainage, they were also the pioneers of cast iron. They hit immediately on the idea of 'democratizing' the washstand and began to produce consoles moulded in one piece, with the feet, mirrors, shelves, soap dishes and towel rails all incorporated into the basic frame, which was completed by the addition of an inset china bowl. These masterpieces of elaborate cast-iron work could be adapted to a variety of styles, from the straight lines of the First Empire to the extravagances of Rococo, and had the very considerable advantage that they were much less expensive than items made by a cabinetmaker. Cast iron was so adaptable that it required no more than a lick of paint to look like marble, wood, bronze or even gold.

After washstands, the manufacturers inevitably turned their attention to the production of baths of the same material, but it was not until the 1880s

This painting (above) shows what a de luxe early twentieth-century bathroom looked like.
The decor is the height of modernity and reflects the theme of water, both in respect of the central pool and in the use of shades of green and blue for the glazed tiles. The room is fitted with a comprehensive range of appliances: to the right, the majestic bathtub, with overhead shower, and the sitz-bath, both in glazed porcelain; in the corner, a shower consisting of a nickel-plated tubular structure fitted with side jets; in an alcove on the left, the bidet and WC, which may be hidden if desired behind a curtain; further along the wall, two washbasins with marble surrounds supported on cabriole legs, one with an articulated shower attachment for washing the face and beard. These two are the only items whose style recalls the time, not long previously, when the washstand was expected to look like a piece of furniture. Apart from the heavy double curtains, everything about this bathroom is in keeping with the model of a modern American bathroom, as shown at the Exhibition of Hygiene in Paris in 1900. Radical in its conception, it placed the accent firmly on hygiene and ease of maintenance.

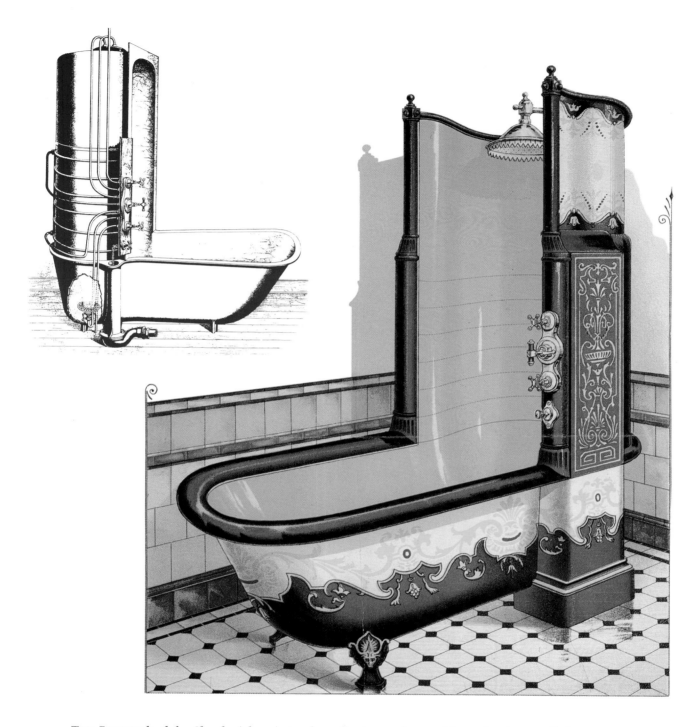

THIS ENGLISH *bath by Shanks (above) stands on lion's paw feet and is made of enamelled cast iron;*
like the shower cabinet mounted at one end, it is painted with decorative motifs. It was this model that took
over at the end of the nineteenth century from the 'sentry-house' bath and shower encased in mahogany
panelling. The section (above, top) shows the mechanism by which water is brought to various points in the
zinc frame, as well as the method by which the bath is filled from the base, and the drainage siphon, an
English invention. In new materials and with modern technology, this hundred-year-old appliance is still the
latest thing for smart private bathrooms – wide rose for the overhead shower spray, side jets and whirlpool bath.
This sumptuous Neo-classical bathroom (pages 128–29) of coloured marble was installed in the late
nineteenth century in the Red Palace, owned by the Holkar family in the town of Indore in India.
Access to the bath is via a large platform and tiers of marble steps or seats, suggesting that it may once
have been used also as a steam bath.

that they had solved all the many problems and were able to make a shell moulded in a single piece that was smooth, of even thickness and not too heavy. The first successful models emerged at much the same time from the Carron and Cockburn factories (in Germany, it was six years later, in France, not until the end of the century). And it was not until the twentieth century that the technical expertise existed to replace the uncomfortable flat surround with a rounded rim and, a few years after that, to perfect the enamelling process. Until then, the paint had tended to wear away under the repeated action of the hot water. The bare iron rusted, and the inside therefore had to be repainted at regular intervals. In *The Diary of a Nobody*, Mr Pooter humorously relates the small inconveniences this caused: 'Painted the bath red, and was delighted with the result.... Bath ready – could scarcely bear it so hot. I per-

severed, and got in; very hot, but very acceptable. I lay still for some time. On moving my hand above the surface of the water, I experienced the greatest fright I ever received in the whole course of my life; for imagine my horror on discovering my hand, as I thought, full of blood. My first thought was that I had ruptured an artery, and was bleeding to death, and should be discovered, later on, looking like a second Marat, as I remember seeing him in Madame Tussaud's. My second thought was to ring the bell, but remembered there was no bell to ring. My third was, that there was nothing but the enamel paint, which had dissolved with boiling water. I stepped out of the bath, perfectly red all over, resembling the Red Indians I have seen depicted at an East-End theatre. I determined not to say a word to Carrie, but to tell Farmerson to come on Monday and paint the bath white.'

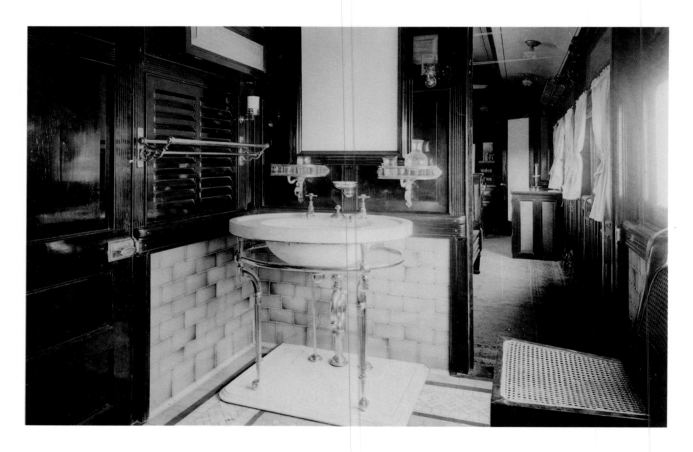

IN TRAINS travelling long distances across the United States, Pullman installed the first wagons-lits with bathrooms in 1865. Economical use of space was the priority, a consideration that did not apply to the fabulous private train consisting of ten compartments that was built in 1905–06 by the East India Railway for the use of the Prince and Princess of Wales on the occasion of their forthcoming trip. The photograph (above) shows the washbasin in the Princess's bathroom – a large porcelain oval receptacle on nickel-plated legs. Today's trend for 'retro' styling has made this type of basin newly fashionable. English models used to be exported all over the world and were for many years unrivalled. There is still a thriving trade in reproductions and cast-iron baths, which have become very popular. In the early 1920s, the bathrooms in the residence of the Maharajah of Dholpur in central India (facing page) were equipped throughout with showers and baths stamped Made in England; *also of English manufacture were the Art Nouveau painted tiles with plant motifs.*

For the external decoration of baths of this type, there was a choice of motifs as extensive as that for English wallpapers. One could have anything from simple gold lines to geometric friezes or armfuls of hand-painted flowers – or you could even create a design of your own.

The change of material for manufacturing baths brought with it a simplification of form, which also influenced the washstand. At first, the wooden or iron frame disappeared altogether, leaving only the marble slab with its inset porcelain basin, the whole mounted on legs – really just a step away from the modern washbasin. In 1900, advertisements began to appear in catalogues for a standard model in china, made in one piece and supported on nickel-plated metal legs, with the basin very similar in shape to that of today. Then came the first pedestal-mounted basins, with their porcelain surfaces covered in floral designs in every conceivable colour, from the blue and white of Delft to riotous profusions of variegated wild flowers. Only very occasionally, as one leafs through the sumptuous catalogues of English manufacturers such as Shoolbred, Doulton and Twyford, does one come across the early models in plain white.

For times were changing, largely under the influence of the United States. By the end of the first decade of the twentieth century, bathrooms all over Europe were tending towards the American model: white, plain, tiled, and no longer seeking to disguise their function. Bathroom appliances and accessories made no attempt to be beautiful. Every metal item was either made of nickel or plated with it – appropriately enough, one may think, given the alternative meaning of 'nickel'. A full bathroom suite in 1902 comprised a washbasin on a nickel-plated stand and a shower with side jets, also made of nickel. The cage was either placed at one end of the bath or – something new – it was a separate installation in a corner of the room, standing above a ceramic base and equipped with a waterproof curtain. It was the Americans who put the high-tech into English comfort and convenience.

By 1900, with the perfection of enamelling processes, such disasters had become a thing of the past. English manufacturers advertised standardized models of baths on 'lion's claw' feet, enamelled inside and painted with lacquer on the outside so that they no longer needed to be boxed in. The heavy mahogany 'sarcophagus and confessional box' went right out of fashion. The new design was altogether lighter and consisted of a bath with claw feet, with a half-cylinder at one end made of a double wall of zinc, pierced with holes on its inside for side and back jets, and surmounted by a large rose to provide the overhead spray. It is the arrangement we still use today for the combined bath and shower.

THIS BATH scene (above) has an element of caricature about it; although it dates from 1905, it can hardly be said to represent the avant-garde of its day. The bath is lavishly ornamented; the bath sheet is dripping with lace; the stool, mules, carpet, armchair, heavy drape, ornamental tiles and the exaggerated gesture of the bather are all reminiscent of a scene staged for some picture postcard of a bygone age, where the bathroom is meant to be 'tasteful' and the act of bathing something vaguely daring. Even more overblown is this marble bath (facing page) with a tinned copper lining that graced one of the bathrooms at the Hôtel Majestic, which opened its doors in Paris in 1905 (as might be guessed from the Art Nouveau style of the tiled friezes). The bath itself is actually much earlier as it came from the Palais de Castille (Hôtel Basiliewsky), which was pulled down when the new hotel was built; it had been the Paris home of Queen Isabella of Spain, who lived there in exile from 1868 onwards.

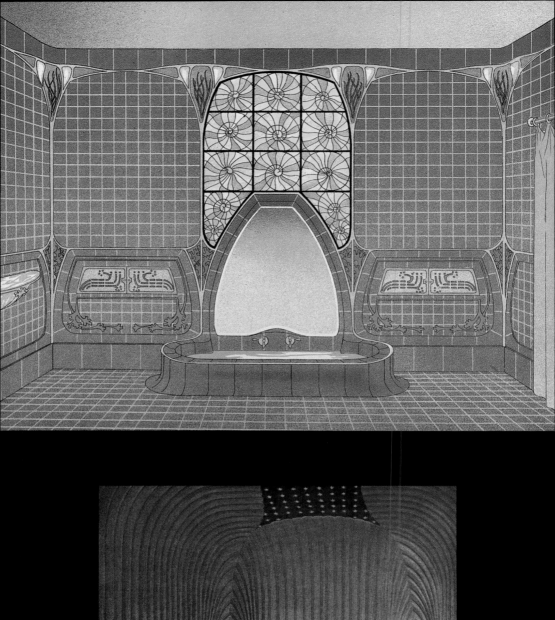

WHITE, CLEAN AND TILED: THE AMERICAN HIGH-TECH BATHROOM

If the English were the champions of the comfortable bathroom in the nineteenth century, it was the Americans who led the way in the twentieth. Approaching the problem from a completely different angle, they devised a room whose elements were mass-produced, with no concern for what they looked like beyond that they should fulfil their primary function of hygiene. It was George Vanderbilt who was the trailblazer, even before the turn of the century, with his revolutionary new design for a technical, functional bathroom. Technical, because the plumbing was reorganized and grouped together along one wall, and functional because it was stripped down to the elements essential for cleanliness, all set out in a row: bath, washbasin mounted on a metal stand and water closet. What is more, it could be installed in a restricted space. The only luxury was the porcelain bathtub, looking very much as it was in the English bathroom, but by now perfected.

Yet the invention of the standard American bathroom adjacent to the bedroom (the model on which our own is based) actually has its roots in the development of a design intended to be used in hotels, later taken up and adapted with a greater or lesser degree of luxury for use in people's homes. As the architect Jefferson Williamson pointed out in 1930, it was through staying in hotels that Americans first encountered bathrooms, hot and cold water and the WC, perhaps the most important of the many such innovations that percolated from the hotel experience into mainstream American life.

In 1829, the Tremont House in Boston was the first hotel to have bathrooms and WCs with running water in its basement. A great leap forward was made in 1853, when the Mount Vernon Hotel at Cape May, a New Jersey resort, offered all rooms with a bath. (It was not until 1906 that the Ritz in Paris could match this.) At the same time, as architects began to favour the minimalist bathroom, so it was brought gradually within reach of increasing numbers of ordinary people.

The decisive moment was the opening of the Startler Hotel in Buffalo in 1908, which advertised a room with its own bathroom for one and a half dollars. The sign caused a sensation, let alone the design. For the first time it was shown that a bathroom did not have to abut on an outside wall as long as proper provision was made for plumbing and ventilation. The system adopted here was to have a block of two symmetrical bathrooms sandwiched between two bedrooms; there was a central shaft for water and ventilation, and in the space left there was room to install fitted wardrobes in each room, flush with the walls.

So was born the notion of the small private bathroom en suite with each of the bedrooms in a private house. That model was gradually to replace the large, English-style family bathroom, which necessitated a trip down the corridor in your dressing gown and the risk of catching cold. It was also better suited to the restricted living space of apartments, which shrank even further with the construction of skyscrapers. Around 1915, in private houses, architects began to range all the appliances along one wall (the English bathtub used to stand alone on the longest wall). In apartments, to create a little more space, the bath would sometimes be turned at right angles, its length dictating the future dimensions of the bathroom.

AT FIRST, bathrooms were done up like tart's parlours, then they were stripped practically bare – the purpose being to show off the wonderful Art Nouveau designs on their glazed ceramic walls. Henri Sauvage and C. Sazarin created this imposing bathroom (facing page, top); revolutionary in conception, it met with incomprehension in 1903, with its huge bath set against a wall of tiling interspersed with decorative panels. Sauvage was one of the first French architects to install shared baths and showers as part of a programme of low-cost housing. There is the same pioneering spirit at work in this room of sublime monastic austerity, designed by H. Will-Wulff in 1902 (facing page, bottom), where the focus of attention is the bath set into a sunken area faced with ceramic tiles. This bathroom (above), although dating from only a few years later, seems suddenly quite Neo-classical, with its bathtub enclosed in an alcove in the antique manner, even though the cast glass on the walls and the two washbasins serve as a reminder of its true date.

All that remained was for the individual elements to be mass-produced – particularly the bathtub, if baths were genuinely to be brought within reach of all pockets. For that to happen however we have to wait until 1916 and the manufacture of a standardized, solid-forged model in enamelled cast iron with double walls, capable of being plumbed in, and with a wall-mounted shower above. By the end of the 1930s, the democratization of the bathroom was truly complete.

The same happened in Britain, original home of the large, mahogany-furnished bathroom. The move towards the American model meant that, even before the First World War, the average middle-class family was able to enjoy the pleasures of bathing at home. After 1919, all new construction undertaken by the State included provision for bathtubs. In 1922, the English novelist and writer W. Somerset Maugham was still able to express the opinion that the morning bath divided society more effectively than birth, wealth or learning, but by the time the 1930s were under way, bathrooms had become sufficiently common in working-class homes to lose those middle-class connotations.

In France, where the minimalist American model was adopted rather later, the bathroom either did not exist at all or it was very much the poor relation, usually sited right at the back of the apartment next to the kitchen and near the water supply. When Jules Verne invented his futuristic bathroom for the Nautilus in *Twenty Thousand Leagues Under the Sea*, it simply did not occur to him to put it anywhere else. Yet, as Pierre Larousse explained in the *Grand Dictionnaire universel*, there was a sense in which people lost out in the changeover to private bathrooms: 'You take your bath in a narrow room, undecorated and without luxury, in one corner of which stands a narrow bath whose water smells only of pipes. When you emerge, no bed to rest on, no massage, no rubs, no oils, a brusque transition from hot to cold: that is the modern bath.'

Members of working-class French households continued for some long time to wash in the kitchen with the aid of bowls, buckets and water jugs. It is worth remembering that in 1911 Henry Provensal,

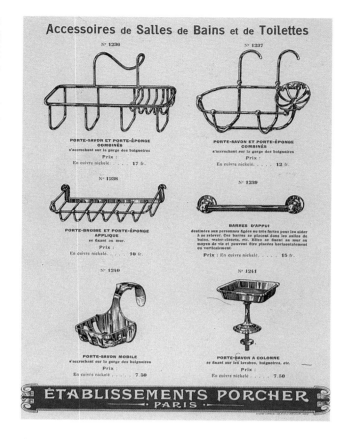

the architect for the Rothschild Foundation, wrote of his dream that one day every dwelling would have a small shower room next to the kitchen, so that working men, mothers and children could pursue a regime of washing daily in warm water without having to set foot outside the home. To us that would not seem much to ask, but at the time it was an impossibly distant dream. Showers were certainly the practical choice, because they saved water and precious square feet. It was the bathtub that came to symbolize the middle-class bathroom. Only luxury blocks with their identical apartments one above the other began to be so equipped from the 1880s onwards, a process which was completed somewhere between 1905 and 1914.

At that time, the market was flooded with 'useful' bathroom accessories. Catalogues have page after page listing a whole inventory of foot-rests and

THIS PHOTOGRAPH of 1884 taken by Paul Nadar shows the bathroom of the young Princess Radziwill (facing page) at a private mansion on the Boulevard de la Tour-Maubourg, Paris. Unusually for a bathroom of that time, it has almost all one could wish in the way of 'modern comforts'. At the start of the twentieth century it would already been out of date, but now, as the twenty-first century dawns, it exerts a peculiar charm. The fireplace, padded couch, cushion and fabric-covered walls are typical of the 'furnished' look of the period. The cheval-glass and the large mirror opposite are reminders that etiquette required a person to check his or her appearance before emerging. The cabinet-style washstand has the traditional matching set of china containers to hold sponges, brushes and other utensils. The splendid Roman-style bath has a large overhead shower rose, but the Princess added a shower 'collar' which she could place on her shoulders to avoid getting her hair wet. Not yet invented were the accessories shown in the Porcher Catalogue of 1905 (above), devised very much with the 'hygienic' bathroom in mind.

IN THE *lavishly produced manufacturers' catalogues of the years 1900 to 1905 (those shown here are for Les Établissements Porcher and Le Grand Dépôt), the old and the new were side by side. There were literally dozens of baths in decorated porcelain, in cast iron, with or without shower, matching bathroom suites in the 'rich' or 'comfortable' ranges: plenty to keep us turning the pages in fascination, exploring a way of life that has gone for ever. The pages for washstands (above) offer the choice between the traditional English wooden cabinet that hides the indiscreet bidet and the foot-bath, or the wall-mounted double washbasin with built-in accessories, which has its plumbing exposed. Finally the illustration (top, right) shows a British fashion of making the new technical appliances look 'artistic', this time by the means of a luxuriant design of birds and flowers.*

bathracks, hooks for hanging up washmitts and horsehair gloves, towel-holders, soap dishes, sponge-holders, toothmug-holders, shelves, small cupboards and clothes stands. There were also ranges of specialized furniture in white lacquer, and in paint (at long last) resistant to steam and water.

It was a mark of the times that bathrooms became both more common and more uniform. All those well-worn injunctions from all sides to keep the home and body clean, coupled with an increasing social pressure, helped finally to tip the balance towards the American-style bathroom. In 1909, the Comtesse de Gencé advocated that a 'gentlewoman' ought to have her bathroom painted with oil-based or enamel paints, which were washable, and recommended getting rid of curtains and rugs that provided a 'breeding-place for germs'. She also urged architects to install the bathroom in a well-aired and well-lit situation near the bedroom. Architects were generally compliant at least as far as furnishing and location were concerned, but in providing windows they were notably less diligent.

The sacrosanct *cabinet de toilette* had continued in existence as long as the bathroom was near the kitchen, but seemed to be rendered obsolete by this change of location. What is more, the new bathroom was no longer a feminine preserve, where the husband had to erase all traces of his presence. But women quickly found a way to reestablish their predominance over the bathroom, at least in the better appointed apartments, by recreating the *cabinet de toilette* as a small en suite bathroom equipped with a washbasin and sometimes a bidet.

Sales rapidly took off. Specialist firms embarked on the manufacture of a vast range of sanitary ware for 'complete *cabinets de toilette* and bathrooms', all mass-produced. The catalogues offered a whole hierarchy of models, from the most luxurious, called the 'rich', to the 'comfortable' and right down to the basic model. From the end of the first decade of the twentieth century, a whole new market existed for everything, up to and including soaps and cosmetics, whose sales were boosted by a barrage of advertisements in the media.

ALBERT GUILLAUME was a painter famous in the early years of the twentieth century for his wickedly amusing sketches of Parisian manners. This scene (above) harks back to an age when the maidservant was still welcome in the cabinet de toilette, *to help her mistress with her bath. The conveniences of the modern bathroom, however, allowed the bath to be taken in complete privacy behind closed doors, a fact alluded to by Célestine in Octave Mirbeau's famous novel* Le Journal d'une femme de chambre: *'I've fallen on my feet ... Madame gets dressed on her own and does her own hair. She locks herself in with a double turn of the key in her* cabinet de toilette, *and I scarcely have the right to set foot inside.... God knows what she does in there for hour after hour!'*

FROM THE NEED TO KEEP CLEAN TO THE PLEASURES OF A COMFORTABLE BATHROOM

In her absorbing study of domestic interiors, *L'Invention de l'habitation moderne*, Monique Eleb traces the development over three consecutive years of advertisements placed by the firm Albert Prost in *L'Illustration* magazine. For a bathroom in the middle market range, the first advertisement of 1909 still harks back to the nineteenth century, with a wash hand-stand and mirror and a copper water heater standing on legs at the foot of the bath. By 1910, the bathroom more or less resembles that of today: the water heater is banished, there is a proper washbasin on a pedestal, a shelf with a mirror above it serves as dressing-table and the bidet makes its appearance. In 1911, while the same photo is used, the slogan has changed. Where the former emphasized the importance of keeping clean ('no health without hygiene'), the second emphasized the pleasures of a comfortable bathroom available 'for an insignificant sum'.

There was enormous interest in this new room that had suddenly become an essential part of every home, whether up-market or mass-market. However cramped the space – even in boats and trains – there had to be a bathroom. It was a huge creative stimulus for architects.

The areas on which they concentrated were plumbing and how it could be simplified, the use of new materials and the experimental prefabrication of some of the elements in order to reduce costs. *Mechanization Takes Command* by Siegfried Giedion, founder of the Congress of Modern Architecture, describes various approaches tried out by the Americans in the 1930s, for example dividing the bathroom into sections, either vertically – the washbasin section being delivered with mirror, shelf and soap dish incorporated – or horizontally, assembled from 'layers' that were screwed together. In 1938, R. Buckminster Fuller invented a complete sealed unit that could be moved around and fitted into the central core of the prefabricated structure of his Dymaxion House. Paradoxically, this would have been the perfect bathroom for Jules Verne's *Nautilus*, but it was less perfect for a house. All the elements and accessories were integral to the floors and walls, and later on Fuller tried to incorporate the kitchen and heating system as well, but it proved simply too limiting to integrate them fully. In the end, the very uniformity of the resulting design proved to be at odds with the freedom and individuality inherent in the notion of building a private house.

These kinds of experiments were in the end to prove more useful for the design of hotel bathrooms. At the same period in France, the leading architects working in this area were Charles-Édouard Jeanneret, better known as Le Corbusier, and Charlotte Perriand. At the 1937 World's Fair, they showed their famous 'cabine sanitaire' for use in hotels. Manufactured by Jacob Delafon, it comprised a washbasin and a WC, which could be transformed into a bidet, while the cabin floor served for the shower. In the 1970s, Charlotte Perriand produced a PVC (thermoplastic resin) version of such a cabin for the winter sports resort of Les Arcs. With the invaluable assistance of a Breton manufacturer of polyester bathroom appliances for use by the navy, she designed a complete bathroom moulded in one piece, delivered ready for installation. This cabin, which you enter via a step, is known to skiers the world over. It consists of a moulded bath, washbasin, shelves and WC, together with all accessories such as lighting. She was also able to export her invention with great success to

DURING THE 1930s, architects and interior decorators were buzzing with new ideas. Never before had bathrooms been so comfortably equipped. Reflecting the lifestyle of a society that placed a premium on personal grooming, and indulged in the worship of the body at thermal spas and on the beach, the space now had to be big enough for exercising. Henri Rapin's design (above) was published in May 1933 in L'Illustration.
Its painted walls combine with glass and mosaic, shiny metal furnishings, light, colour, the large sunken bath, and the tinkling fountain to create a mood of 'liquid' tranquility. The sunken bath is one of the enduring symbols of luxury, a fantasy explored by the cinema on numerous occasions, as in this scene (facing page) from a film entitled Faithless.

the hotels of a country that has a great tradition of bathing, and where space-saving solutions are essential: Japan.

All this is in complete contrast to the lack of progress in respect of the conventional bathroom, whether the de luxe or the standard model, where revolutionary inventions were thin on the ground until about the late 1960s. The exception is the solid-forged bathtub in enamelled cast iron that appeared in the 1920s, and which, according to Siegfried Giedion, achieved 'the level of comfort people had been seeking for more than two thousand years'. There was also the mass-produced bath designed to fit into a corner, and there were ceramic finishes with names like 'jade green', 'black tulip', and 'Dubarry pink'.

This period of inaction corresponded more or less to the time it took for the majority of the Western population to refamiliarize themselves with bathing, and then make the transition from washing in order to keep clean to bathing for pleasure. In this change of attitude, newspapers and magazines proved very influential, as were the cinema and film stars, which, by glamorizing a lifestyle, exerted a very powerful influence on public opinion.

In 1918 Cecil B. De Mille began to introduce bath scenes into his movies, to the vast chagrin of the puritanical critics of his day. Initially these tended to be morally didactic. The bathroom scene might, for example, be used to show the wife's slovenly and untidy behaviour, as the explanation for her husband falling for the charms of an impeccably neat and well turned out young lady. Then, with Gloria Swanson in *Male and Female* (1919), for the first time he made the scene glamorous: silk robe, maids to wait on her, foaming sponges, and a bath like a swimming pool, with steps down into it. By consciously using so many different sequences of this type in his films, as well as so many different styles of bathroom, the director believed he really had exerted a sociological influence on the American population – helping no doubt to influence not just the numbers of bathrooms installed in homes but also their comfort and elegance. And why not, when one considers the number of bath sequences, even in contemporary films, that show the star buried under a mound of luxuriant bubbles, frequently in some exotic bath or setting. Bathtubs would be shaped like waves, shells, swans and even white peacocks, and those vast marble pools of the costume dramas set generation after generation of film-goers dreaming, their fascination only enhanced by representations in glossy magazines of the extravagant bathrooms in the villas of the Hollywood stars.

Two BATHROOMS, two sex symbols of the late 1950s – which would we now think more sexy? In this legendary scene from Billy Wilder's film The Seven Year Itch *(above), the plumber concentrates intently on the taps, while Marilyn Monroe lies buried under a mound of foam, playing with her toes, in a typical 1950s-style bathtub faced with black tiles. In total contrast is the kitsch decorative style (facing page) of the curvaceous Jayne Mansfield's bathroom, with its pink shag-pile carpet and gilded heart-shaped bath.*

THE PERFECTLY EQUIPPED MODERN BATHROOM

'All kinds of pots on a white basin, towels made of soft material, eau de Cologne; a bathtub you could sit in, you turned on a tap and the water ran cold, and from the other one it ran hot ...' This was the description of a young girl from Lille, Lise Vanderwielen, in *Lise du plat pays*, of a bathroom in Brussels in the 1920s that sounds as if it was equipped with everything necessary to make bathing a pleasure. We might be tempted to think that we have not advanced very much beyond that, but there are in fact two main things that separate our contemporary bathroom from that one in Brussels: technology and aesthetics.

'All kinds of pots on a white basin,' exclaims Lise.

That basic white model has never really gone out of fashion, and yet of all the bathroom appliances, it is the washbasin that is now being subjected to multiple reinterpretations. It might have been thought impossible to improve upon, so perfectly was its form adapted to its function. But in the last few years it has been entirely redesigned and has reemerged as a free-standing unit with a central structure integrating conduits for plumbing and electricity, enabling it to be placed anywhere. Designers have elevated it to the status of a cult object, dedicated to the daily ritual of our ablutions, its aesthetic so refined as to make it as much an item of sculpture as a functional object.

The classic washbasin continues to be made in glazed fire-proof porcelain (as of necessity are the bidet and WC), which is resistant to acids and other chemicals. The handsome pre-war model of the pure-white, pedestal-mounted basin seems set to continue for a good few years yet, but increasingly people are tempted by colour, by basins that are wall-mounted or inset, and by synthetic materials. Reflecting a change in washing habits, double basins are no longer always situated side by side – the traditional arrangement that permitted a certain shared intimacy while washing in the same room.

Only a minority of paying customers look to original models by architects and interior decorators or find out what the big-name designers have to offer. This may be anything from a round basin on a central base, reminiscent of the ancient Greek *louterion* used for ritual purification, to a reinterpretation of the elegant console incorporating storage cupboard, shelves, mirror, towel racks and devices to hold glasses and toothbrushes, transformed by some new feature or by the use of new materials (aluminium, stainless or polished steel, glass, or new types of thermoplastic resin).

There are the sublime washbasins produced by Philippe Starck and Andrée Putman, Finn Skœdt's audacious watertowers, basins with interchangeable pedestals by Dieter Sieger, Marc Sadler's amusing 'totems', with all the various appliances attached to a modular column. Occasionally the washbasin even becomes an art object in its own right, as at the 'European Capitals of the New Design' exhibition of 1991, which included Elisabeth Lux's design for a basin set into a sheet of sanded glass, with subtle touches of stainless steel, gilt brass and mirror glass.

Lise made no mention of a bidet. This is not so surprising when you remember the associations of its dubious past. Only during the 1930s did the bidet begin to lose its immodest reputation and even today, in countries where it is a perfectly familiar object, mentioning it seems somehow out of place,

THE EXUBERANT Roman-style decor of this early twentieth-century bathroom (above) is created by the use of countless small tiles of cast glass imported from Italy, covering everything from floor to ceiling, including the walls, the bath, the basin in its alcove and the console. The material is designed to withstand the humid heat of a system of circulating hot water, almost like that of the hammam, which is concealed within the columns on either side of the basin. Compare this with the antiseptic good order of the respectable bourgeois environment captured in this photograph by Robert Doisneau (facing page). The spotless white tiles and milky-white basin, the sparkle of the chrome, the glass and the crystal and silver toilet set, all serve to focus the light on the face of the maid, whose disenchanted gaze is caught in the shimmering reflection of the lid and the hand mirror. Note the pedestal washbasin with its cut-off corners and cross-style taps, one of the most popular 'retro' models on sale today.

provoking an amused smile, a polite silence or out-right disapproval.

Traditionally its use has been confined to the Latin peoples of Europe (as well as parts of southern Germany), while the Anglo-Saxons have shunned it. In the United States, before the Second World War, the Ritz Hotel in New York actually dared install bidets in its bathrooms, but was obliged to remove them because of the moral outrage they aroused. The liner *Normandie* was forced to take the same decision in respect of its first-class accommodation.

Today, the United States remains implacably against bidets, although in England there are stirrings of interest. The French themselves more or less abandoned the bidet twenty years ago. Significantly, it no longer forms part of the minimum standards for bathrooms in local authority tower blocks, and today's teenagers have little or no idea what this object

is for. However, a new market has opened up in the Middle East, to which exports are healthy, and for the hypercritical who deplore its lack of beauty, it will soon be possible to buy a model integral with the WC, of the type already used in luxury hotels.

'A bathtub you could sit in,' said Lise. At that period, it would already have been made of enamelled cast iron and would therefore have felt comfortable against the skin. It might have been the old model, which stood on four feet, high enough to bathe sitting down and slightly flared in shape for ease of movement, or it might possibly have been the latest model available in 1920, which was longer and lower, and enabled the bather to lie back as it was sloped at one end.

Even today, with all its advantages and disadvantages, enamelled cast iron remains the best choice. Expensive, heavy and rather cold to the touch when empty, it alone retains heat. It is also a good insulator against sound, resists wear and tear, and stays shiny and clean for years.

Here and now in the twentieth century, what would be the bath of people's dreams? Would it be a Jacuzzi made of a synthetic material, in which you could give vent to your mermaid fantasies, or would it be an antique or reproduction model in marble, stone or copper, in which you could take your ease in the style of Poppea, Gabrielle d'Estrées, La Pompadour or Pauline Bonaparte? For sheer modernity, you would certainly opt for the bathtub in a synthetic material, which is undoubtedly the bath of the twenty-first century. The acrylic bathtub was invented in England in the early 1980s. It is light and strong (if it takes a knock it can easily be pressed back into shape), warm to the touch even when empty, keeps the water hot reasonably well and is naturally non-slip. The most adaptable of materials, it can be of any colour, whether the two hundred or so that are commercially available or your personal choice – anything from the colour of your comfort blanket when you were a child to that of the motif on the tiles you brought back from Morocco. There is even the option of a faithful reproduction of the Venus in your life, a detail of the frescoes from the Sistine Chapel or creatures from the depths of the

MARBLE IS the traditional material for the very finest bathrooms. Although some would argue that it is cold to the touch, its veiny sheen looks wonderful against shimmering water and it feels as soft as skin. Pink veined with black was the choice of English industrialist Frank Parkinson for the country house called Charters (above) he had built in 1938. In Hollywood movies, marble baths are almost a cliché, given the frequency with which they occur. The point is that they look lavish and expensive. What is different about the marble bath in Otto Preminger's legendary 1944 film Laura *(facing page, top) is its location, right in the middle of the office of a journalist who likes to write his copy in the bath. In George Cukor's* The Women *(facing page, bottom), released in 1939, the bath itself is remarkable as it is made entirely of crystal. Joan Crawford lies there making interminable treacherous phone calls from her white telephone, which sits on a curious sort of tray with adjustable mirror that sits across the bath.*

arm rests. At each end is a soft head rest, one end sloped for reclining, the other designed for sitting upright. And most recent of all, there is the combination bath. At the head end it is like a bath, while at the foot there is a proper cylindrical shower space with a movable glass partition; the space is sometimes equipped with a seat on which to perch while giving yourself a pedicure.

For those without the time to soak in a bath there are the pleasures of a brisk shower. In France, at the turn of the century, the Baronne de Staffe was already enthusing over the new handheld models, in the style of a crescent, a circle or a crinoline. It was the last that seemed to find particular favour: 'a darling of a shower, elegant in invention, a genuine delight; a real dew caresses you like a quilt of the finest down.'

For a long time regarded as the choice of the working classes, no more than an inferior substitute for the middle-class bathtub, the shower has again become fashionable. It has always been recognized and recommended for its invigorating qualities, and it is probably because of sport that it has been taken up with such enthusiasm recently. After physical

South Sea oceans – all hand-painted on the outside of your transparent shell.

More seriously, thanks to synthetic materials manufacturers have been able to produce different shapes designed for ever great comfort. Large bathtubs for multiple occupation, corner baths for ease of installation, double baths with shower as well as bath: they come in all shapes, sizes and depths. If you are concerned to save energy, you have no need to follow the example of King George VI of Great Britain, who during the Second World War determined to save water by painting a sort of red Plimsoll Line on the inside of his bath.

Whatever their size, contemporary baths are extremely comfortable. The taps work easily – no more big toes pressed into service – the telescopic shower attachment is fully retractable – goodbye to the dangling hose that gets tangled up and then splits. And if the ergonomically designed shapes of the interiors at first look pointless or far-fetched you should be aware that these include foot rests appropriate for child and medium or large adult, according to where you position yourself. Halfway up there are

AFTER THE introduction in the early 1920s of the solid-forged bathtub in enamelled cast-iron (above, bottom), which, to quote the architect and commentator Siegfried Giedion, represented 'the level of comfort people had been seeking for more than two thousand years', very few significant improvements in bathroom appliances occurred before the 1950s. The only exception was that baths were mass-produced in different sizes and included a model designed to fit neatly into a corner (above, top). Combined with the large square pedestal washbasin, it formed a duo of 'charm and distinction' as the English manufacturer Ideal Standard boasted in its promotional literature of 1951 and 1953, 'guaranteeing that they met the standards of robustness and hygiene required by the modern bathroom'.

exertion, people tend to prefer showers to baths as a way of waking up and getting moving. In addition, in a society where saving time has become almost as much of an obsession as personal grooming, the shower is perfect for early weekday mornings, the bath for lazy evenings and weekends.

Experts have estimated at over seventy per cent the proportion of people who have changed over from baths to showers, something made possible by the wide availability of the hand shower attachment, mounted against the wall on a sliding bar, and

with a small, round showerhead. Undoubtedly this contraption has helped to transform the weekly bath into the daily shower. Its pleasures were considerably enhanced in 1968 by the invention of the famous ergonomically designed 'Selecta' shower, with the little square holes that enabled the force of the jet to be adjusted with a simple twist of the showerhead. An invention of genius by the German firm Hansgrohe, this has sold more than seventeen million units to date. Most current models of shower attachments have three adjustable jets and

THE OCCUPANT (above) of this standard model corner bath, obviously a size too small, is the debonair Gary Cooper, so often cast in films as the average male American. Here he is shown relaxing in the bath after reading the papers in Cecil B. De Mille's 1944 film The Story of Dr Wassell. *Where the female bath was often an excuse for 'glamour' shots, the male bath – the occupant often fully clothed – was usually intended to make you laugh. One thinks immediately of Laurel and Hardy, Buster Keaton and Groucho Marx with his trademark cigar, then later on Kirk Douglas and Henry Fonda, grinning away in their wooden tubs in Mankiewicz's* There was a Crooked Man *(1970), Tony Curtis and Monroe in* Some Like It Hot *(1959) and Peter Sellers in* The Party *(1968), not to mention the legendary bath scene with Dustin Hoffman in* Little Big Man *(1970) or Mick Jagger's bath in* Performance *(1970) in the company of some charming young friends.*

are designed to use less water, without any detectable loss of performance.

But as everyone knows, the real delight is to take a shower not in the bath but in a cubicle behind a glass door with a proper wall-mounted shower. The sheer joy of the pure jetting water is unsurpassed. Built according to your desired dimensions in tiles or little mosaic pieces, it represents the height of aesthetic and personal pleasure. But even preformed cubicles with no aesthetic appeal whatsoever are extremely comfortable. They come in all shapes and sizes, with hand showers, overhead showers and integral bench seats, and they can be packed up and taken with you when you move.

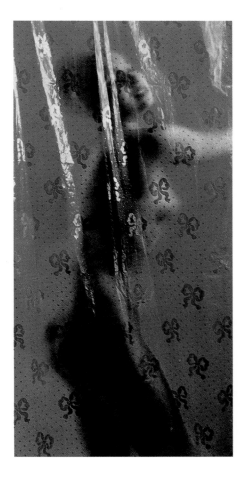

It seems we have everything we need to surrender ourselves to the enjoyment of water – or almost everything, for you need to be certain of a constant flow of water at an even temperature if you are not to experience the horrors of what has been called the 'Scottish' shower, which runs hot and cold without rhyme or reason. How could we manage today without a constant supply of hot water?

'You turned on a tap and the water ran cold, and from the other one it ran hot,' Lise went on, wonderstruck by this miracle. For us, hot water seems no big deal, and yet it could not exist without the gas that was piped into people's homes to replace the burning of coal and wood, which were dirty, and methylated spirits, which was hazardous. The first gas water heaters appeared in 1851 or thereabouts. There were a few minor explosions at the start, but substantial improvements around 1870 made it possible to heat a given volume of water at reasonable speed as and when it was needed, and also to maintain a constant temperature by means of an invention called the thermostat. Originally cylindrical and made of copper and brass, with a round gas burner at the base, the new heater provided water for a hot bath in one hour, while behind a door in the top part of the appliance was a space where you could put the bath towels to get warm, enabling you to dry yourself in comfort. It was an overnight success. In 1907 alone, the Porcher company sold more than eighty-two thousand units. The cylindrical model was subsequently altered to an oblong shape that could easily be attached to the wall. Having hot water on tap made an enormous difference in terms of privacy, since it dispensed with the need for a maidservant to be present. 'All you needed was a match, and in the time it took you to get undressed, your bath or shower was ready.'

With advances in plumbing, the water-heating appliance could be physically removed from the bathroom. As if by magic, water would arrive from some distant part of the house, often from the supply heated by the big kitchen stove or coal-burning kitchen range. An advertisement appeared in *L'Illustration* in 1939 in praise of the coal-burning Aga, which could heat a tank of hot water in four minutes and let you have a bath for forty centimes, 'the price of a cigarette'. The accompanying picture showed a woman in an elegant dressing-gown, nonchalantly dangling a cigarette as she trailed the fingers of one hand in the water of her running bath. Later came the all-purpose water heater, to supply the central heating as well as the hot water cylinder

AN EXEMPLARY simplicity characterizes these designs (facing page) by Philippe Starck for the German firms of Duravit, Hansgrohe and Hoesch. The old-fashioned pan or bowl is transformed into a shower base. The shallow basin of antiquity, into which the water flowed with a beautiful circular motion, is reinterpreted here for the modern washbasin. Just like the old portable bath vat, the bathtub now occupies the centre of the room, surrounded by a chrome-plated rail for towels. The shape of the bidet and WC is reminiscent of the galvanized iron bucket, and the washstand in pearwood that of a barrel. And finally, the old hand-pump provides the inspiration for the mixer tap, the action of its slender handle echoing that familiar forward and back movement. A perfect illustration of the joy of surrendering oneself to water is this photograph of a young woman in the shower, taken by Paul Outerbridge in the early 1940s (above). The pattern of bows on the curtain provides a slightly bizarre counterpoint to the well-toned body it partially conceals.

(originally it was coal- or oil-fired, then heated by gas or electricity).

Later in the twentieth century, the connection became still more tenuous – and the distance travelled by the hot water even greater – for a single power source might serve a block of flats, or even a whole town; the power might also come from solar panels.

Last but not least important of bathroom appliances are the taps: technical miracles in miniature. The modern tap is made up of more than forty parts and has to pass innumerable tests to ensure it can withstand the thousands of rotations to which it will be subjected in the course of a year.

'Robinet', the French word for a tap, owes its name to a type of sheep that in the Middle Ages was called a *robin* – there is a mention of it in Rabelais. The very first French taps were often made in the shape of a small sheep's head, giving rise to the diminutive form *robinet*. The quarter-turn system (the tap or spigot used for casks and barrels) has been known since antiquity. The Romans made such a tap in lead (also wood, tin and bronze), giving it a conical barrel with a hole that could be placed in the open or shut position; it was frequently decorated with animal designs. Lead taps were made for many centuries, but the material was incapable of withstanding the pressure of water used to supply the taps of the industrial age. From 1870, taps were therefore made of brass with a full-turn screw joint, packed to ensure that it was watertight. In the 1930s, bathroom taps tended to be plated with nickel or chrome. Today our modern tap is equipped with ceramic valves and uses a quarter- or half-turn mechanism. The exterior is chrome-plated or covered in a plastic material available in a variety of colours.

The concept of the mixer tap goes back at least to the Roman Empire, although it is only recently that it has been widely available for washbasins. Until the late 1950s, it was used only by a minority who preferred to wash in running water. For everyone else with two taps, it was still necessary to fill up the washbasin with water in the time-honoured way.

True modernity arrived with the first advanced mixer tap manufactured in 1972 by Ideal Standard. With a single gesture in two dimensions it was possible to achieve whatever temperature you desired. And with the thermostatically controlled mixer tap, which enables the temperature to be pre-set to within a single degree, absolute comfort is now assured. Once the perfect temperature has been chosen, it will remain exactly the same however often the taps are used.

Ease of use, perfect comfort and technical excellence, with the aim of making life as safe and as simple as possible: that is essentially the credo that has governed the development of bathroom appliances during this century. We shall see how in the same period their form too has evolved, and how people have chosen to display them within the very private space of the bathroom.

THIS SHOWER (facing page) by the German manufacturer Hansgrohe has sold more than seventeen million to date. When it was introduced in 1968, it revolutionized the lives of the growing army of shower enthusiasts, banishing for ever those thin trickles of water that dribbled from the limescale-clogged traditional shower. The little round perforations in the rose of the classic shower were replaced by a ring of holes that were square in section, enabling the power of the jet to be adjusted with a simple twist of the showerhead. Current, technically advanced models usually have three types of adjustable jet and are designed to use less water without any detectable loss of performance.

FROM ART DECO TO THE CONTEMPORARY BATHROOM

The decor of the luxury bathroom echoes twentieth-century trends in interior decoration in general. In the Art Nouveau period, baths were set into alcoves and encased within china panels; washbasins and bidets were of glazed stoneware in the shape of waves or shells, lavishly decorated with multi-coloured reliefs. Sometimes even the 'fiery steed' so beloved of Colette would be transformed into a Wagnerian swan. The decor might be a riot of luxuriant foliage and flowers, or it might be a sea-scape with pebbles, shells and seaweed coiling round the long-haired sea-nymphs that encircled the bath.

The break came in the early 1920s, when an incipient sobriety signalled the rise of Art Deco. Among the most famous bathrooms of this period was that designed by the architect Armand Rateau for the great couturier Jeanne Lanvin. Antique in inspiration, but highly stylized, it features a contrast between the geometric design of the floor in coloured marble with the gentle ovals of the bathroom appliances, using wrought iron for many of the decorative details and for all the accessories, including the taps with their elegant bird silhouettes. The bath is in an alcove, the back wall of which is decorated with a bas-relief on the theme of birds in trees. There is a reconstruction of this exquisite room in the permanent collections of the Musée des Arts Décoratifs in Paris.

During the 1930s, the quest for comfort and beauty attained perfection, with the result that the Art Deco style continued to be used for bathroom appliances until well beyond the Second World War. It still provides inspiration for the designers of today. The opulent 1930s bathroom is the expression of everything Madame de Gencé ever dreamed of at the turn of the century: spacious and light, and situated near the bedroom.

Designs by the interior decorators and architects of the period reflected the lifestyle of a privileged class that, today, has become the norm. The lessons of the hygienists had been absorbed, and people began to keep fit, playing sports, practising gymnastics (the bathroom was adjacent to a space for physical exercise), as well as visiting spas or so-called health resorts and taking holidays by the sea, where people undressed on the beach. In town, fashion decreed shorter skirts and plunging necklines, and slit skirts that showed off the legs, which now had to be tanned. This was the ideal woman, as seen in the 800,000 copies of *Marie-Claire* distributed in 1937. A new woman, impeccably turned out, who therefore needed to spend long hours in the bathroom getting ready.

In a 1931 catalogue of the prestigious Société de Fonderie, the writer Pierre Mac Orlan gave his definition of modern comfort and beauty: '1931-style comfort has supplied the aesthetic for domestic life in 1931.... For the first time it is function that creates decor and imposes a decorative clarity upon it, rather than the decor imposing its own arbitrary caprices on the objects it envelops.... The human eye is becoming accustomed to the noble simplicity of lines and objects. [Before that] our eyes clung jealously to ancient images of decor that safeguarded nothing unless it be a tradition of purely mental comfort.'

Interior decorators and architects were working

THIS FABULOUS shower (above) has a distinguished history. It is part of the Hollywood-style bathroom that once belonged to the Maharani of Rajasthan in her suite at the palace of Jodhpur; started in 1929, it took fifteen years to construct. All the furnishings and accessories that had been ordered from England were torpedoed by German warships, so everything had to be made by local craftsmen 'in the style of' the original. The bathroom is clad entirely in marble, while the bath is of onyx and set into an alcove, which is gilded like the shower. The palace was turned into a hotel in 1977. Less ostentatious but equally splendid is the bathroom that belonged to the couturier Jeanne Lanvin (facing page), designed for her by the interior decorator Armand Rateau in 1923. It is in the Greek antique manner, but highly stylized. The geometric designs on the coloured marble floor are cleverly combined with the gentle ovals of appliances carved out of yellow marble. Black wrought iron is used for the decorative elements, consisting of elegant silhouettes of birds in profile. The wonders of this bathroom can still be admired today in the permanent collections of the Musée des Arts Décoratifs, Paris.

AMERICAN ART DECO (facing page) is the style of this bathroom in the Chanin Building, New York,
designed by Jacques Delamarre. Although utilitarian and uncluttered, in the manner approved since the
beginning of the century, it is nevertheless luxurious. The tiles were custom-made and based on ancient Egyptian
motifs, while the lighting and heating are the most technically advanced of their day. The French Art Deco style
in shades of silver was used for the bathroom of the Minister of Foreign Affairs at the Palais d'Orsay (above),
designed by Ruhlmann. Like the handbasin, the bath glitters with mother-of-pearl mosaic. Above the bath
is a crystal swan made by Lalique, while the cupboard with its wonderful marquetry and mother-of-pearl
inlay was also designed by the famous decorator. Gilded like the surface of the sea at sunset,
the colours of the cast glass motifs of this fabulous bathroom in Bordeaux (pages 156–57) represent a
magisterial rebuttal of the notion of the bathroom as a high-tech space dedicated to hygiene!

along much the same lines. Some, in the pursuit of comfort, were to make their designs timeless, others were avant-garde as much in their concept of the bathroom as in their use of materials – Pierre Chareau, René Herbst, Le Corbusier and Frank Lloyd Wright being among the leading representatives of the latter tendency.

Interior decoration magazines of the time, as well as more recent monographs, offer a veritable treasure trove of illustrations of private bathrooms by the top designers. Architects such as Franck and Ruhlmann used plain but sumptuous materials: veined marble for the walls, black or white marble for the bath and washbasin, travertine, granite panels, mirrors set into chrome or nickel-plated metal or bronze, marquetries of cast glass and mirror glass, and frosted glass by great artists such as Daum and Lalique. The architect Pierre Chareau used wood to create a 'Japanese' atmosphere, with cupboards, stools and shower base all in teak; for his sublime Glass House in Paris he employed 'industrial' materials such as frosted glass, which he used for partitions and the curving wall of a shower, as well as Duralumin, aluminium and white tiles, with granito or tiles of natural rubber for the floors.

At the Salon d'Automne of 1934, the architect René Herbst showed his famous ocean liner cabin, a masterpiece of economy and functionality: a cylinder in nickel-plated metal to contain the shower and its accessories, a washbasin suspended inside a column of tubular steel, with attached glass-holder, soap dish and mirror. For the Villa Savoye, Le Corbusier 'built' a shower and bathtub of cast glass tiles, with an elevated area at the end for an integral reclining chair of the same material. The architect also did a great deal of work on mass housing schemes and sanitation: in the plans for the Cité Radieuse in Marseille, completed in 1952, he adopted the pattern of a family bathroom with washbasins in adjoining bedrooms.

SHOWN HERE are two contrasting bathrooms designed by Pierre Chareau during the 1930s. A leading member of the architectural avant-garde, in his Glass House in Paris (top) he opted for austerity: grey cast glass, industrial materials and frosted glass screens so as not to break up the space or block the light, with a spacious shower and huge bath installed behind them. As a decorator, he chose the sober luxury of teak – heavy and impervious to rot – in this Japanese-influenced bathroom (bottom) which is designed to be comfortable as well as good-looking.

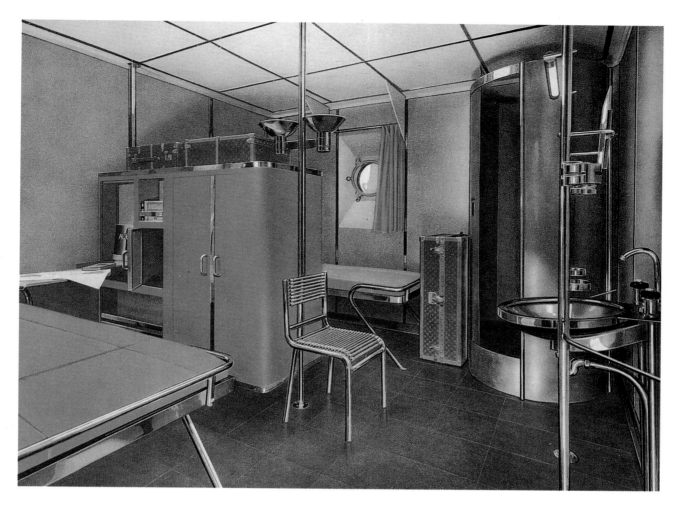

For France, as far as bathrooms in general were concerned, the 1940s and 1950s were very much the time for catching up with the neighbours. In the old apartment blocks where there had been no provision for them, people either had to sacrifice a whole room or squeeze one into an odd corner. In new blocks of rented flats, they tended to be of the minimum standard. Bathing as a pleasurable experience was still a distant prospect. Everyone was trying to fit the bathtub into the smallest possible space; there was even a design for a washbasin with the plumbing on a pivot, so that it could be tucked away into the bath space after use; the bidet too was pivoted. Only in exceptional circumstances was any attention paid to how it all looked. The bathroom was an unimportant place that made you feel nothing in particular. It was just the place where you washed, more to be clean than for any pleasure.

We have to wait for the late 1960s, and the rapid transformations that overtook Western society, for bathrooms also to begin to change. Cautious attempts by designers such as Gae Aulenti and Andrée Putman began to find enthusiasm among their clientele, and the use of new materials such as thermoplastic resin pointed the way ahead for the 1970s. It was actually in 1969 that Joe Colombo designed for the 'Interzum' exhibition in Cologne a house 'of the third kind', with a bathroom for family use, all the

ANOTHER PIONEERING talent of the 1930s was René Herbst, who caused a sensation at the Salon d'Automne of 1934 with his 'ocean liner cabin' bathroom (above). It still looks as modern today and continues to inspire designers, with its sliding-door cylinder to house the shower, and washbasin mounted on a tubular steel column, with holders and containers for soap, glass, and so on all attached, all made of nickel steel.

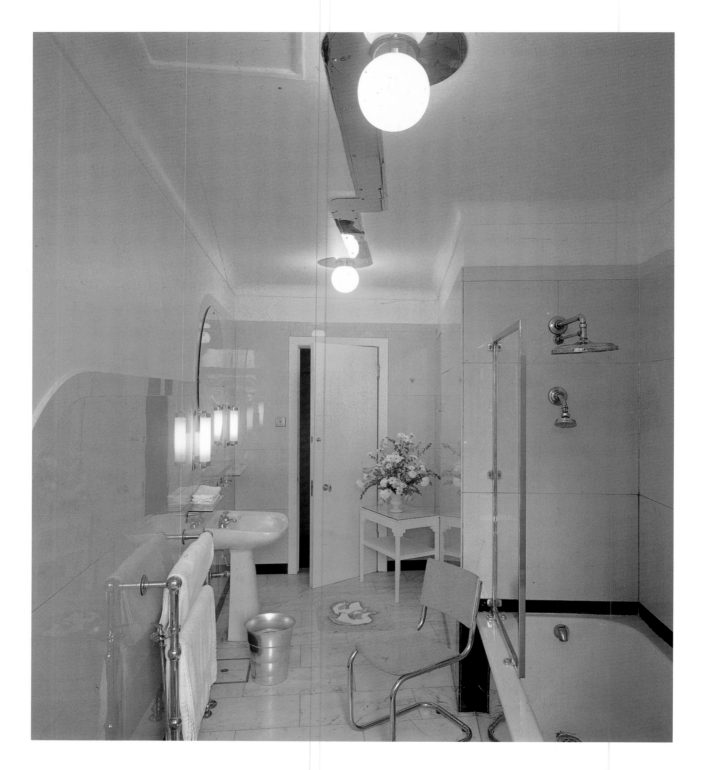

WHAT COULD *be more pleasant on arrival at your hotel, when you have put down your luggage,*
than to dive into the bathroom and run yourself a bath – a familiar and reassuring sound that at once makes
you feel at home. In the annexe to Claridge's in London, designed by Oswald Milne in 1930, the legendary
service and comfortable bathrooms ensure an immediate sense of well-being. Quite unlike the nightmare of
staying at one of those impersonal places – literally with no personnel at all – described in Truismes, *the novel*
by Marie Durrieussecq: 'I put a ticket in a machine and received a sort of magnetic card which opened the door
of the room and that of the bathroom.' An archetypal post-Art Deco installation (facing page), in respect of
the colours of the tiles and of the appliances, this Paris bathroom has everything needed to make bathing
a pleasure: light, space, comfort – and fluted columns to lend a spice of the exotic.

elements of which were made of moulded PVC. A large shower and bath were incorporated, along with their taps and accessories, in a sphere two metres in diameter, all very much in the spirit of Stanley Kubrick's film *2001: A Space Odyssey*.

All the seventies designs were about a new way of living, a new way of inhabiting the family space. Yet behind the futuristic and Utopian exteriors, and in spite of all the aluminium, laminates and plastics that were used to create radical new shapes, the bathroom was becoming a place for the expression of feelings. The colours – orange, maroon, fuchsia and violet – were significant: invigorating, to put you in the right mood, or psychedelic, so that you could just float away as you lay in the bath, with a soft carpet to put your feet on, cushions, music and, for the first time, green pot plants to lend atmosphere.

It was during the 1980s, when almost everyone had a bathroom, that people seriously began to want to make their own bathroom different, an indicator of who they were in the social and cultural scheme of things. For this new clientele, large manufacturers of sanitary ware devised a strategy of 'designer' ranges. The couturier Courrèges was the first to design a new line for Allia. Since then many firms have used designers: Colani at Villeroy and Boch, Enzo Mari and Paolo Tilche at Ideal Standard, Laufen at Porsche Design, Matteo Thun at Allia, and many more. There has been an increasing move away from traditional shapes. One of the more striking examples is the 'back to basics' bathroom designed by Philippe Starck for Duravit, with its bath vats from a bygone age and the good old-fashioned buckets that have been used for centuries to carry water – while his basin standing on a table could in the blink of an eye be transformed into the familiar basin on a washstand.

At the same time, the embellishment of the bathroom is evidence of an important shift in thinking: a desire, certainly, to prolong the narcissistic pleasures of personal grooming in an agreeable environment, but also a desire to be sociable and to share the space with other family members. The last great bastion of privacy has now become simply another room in the apartment, one that people are happy for visitors to see, since it has been decorated with as much care as the sitting room.

THE HOTEL bathroom is an interesting area for experiment, because of the heterogeneous and rapidly changing clientele that must be catered for. It is a exercise in style that some of the most talented young designers have explored in recent years. Andrée Putman was one of the first, with her designs for the Morgan Hotel in New York. Her black and white chessboard decor (facing page) is familiar the world over, as is her ultra-simple washbasin in chrome steel. A new twist on the traditional washstand is this design for the Hôtel de la Cour des Loges in Lyon by Philippe Starck, shown here (above) in the version made in tubular chrome steel. Standing solidly on its legs, skirted by towels, it seems to reach out to welcome, its two little dishes for the soap like two hands reaching towards you, its bevelled mirror returning your gaze.

Bathroom layouts have now reached the second generation. This is the time for renovation or for installing a second bathroom. New habits need to be accommodated, requiring new amenities: baths big enough for two to share, proper shower cabinets, a second washbasin, even the separate installation of a spacious shower room, usually reserved for the head of the household. In Italy and Germany, people spend most money on their bathrooms. Visitors get shown over them in the way that a few years ago they would have been proudly shown the new kitchen. On the one hand, the bathroom is an indicator of wealth, but it is also the place in which one invests the most of oneself, a reflection not only of the importance of the cult of the body in society in

A STARKLY alien mineral landscape – concrete, granite, marble, glass and steel – characterizes these temples to water. The most extraordinary is the 'crypt' (above, top), which was designed in 1991 by the Japanese architect Massakazu Bokura for a penthouse apartment in Paris owned by a compatriot. The walls and floor are clad in Lauhelin granite (like the Cour de Napoléon at the Palais du Louvre). The bath of curved glass is a masterpiece of new technology by Guillaume Saalburg and Patrick Desserme. The alternate bands of flecked and transparent glass are supposed to represent bamboo. Using the simplest volumes and geometric shapes (above, bottom), the space occupied by the bath and the shower is subdivided into a series of rectangular blocks, while the expansive forms of the cylinder and the circle are the repeated leitmotivs in the bathroom designed by Kripacz (facing page) for Erickson House, on the ocean front outside Los Angeles.

general but of your own view of yourself. For that reason, it is difficult to make generalizations about the contemporary look.

Certainly one of the major trends in decoration, and possibly the most significant, is what the professionals call 'retro', that somewhat nostalgic temptation to turn the bathroom into a fully furnished room. Of course, this is no longer because we fear being 'overcome with boredom', as at the end of the nineteenth century; it is because we want to make the room look lived in, reflecting the amount of time we spend in it (more than ten hours a week on average for women, a little less for men).

The most popular choices are the styles of the late eighteenth century, the Empire period and 1900–30. The bathroom, the most recent addition to the dwelling space, has finally discovered its roots. People are installing old furniture, reclining beds, period accessories, basins and baths – the good, old-fashioned, deep cast-iron bath standing on its four feet being the most frequent choice. The point is to create an atmosphere, something manufacturers of sanitary ware entirely neglected when the bathroom entered the era of mass-production.

The other strong trend is for a space that takes its inspiration from watery themes – whether in the spirit of postmodernism or 'back to basics'. The sole common denominator here is in the rigorous use of materials. On the one hand, the plainness of metal and frosted glass, combined with greys and greens suggesting cool natural streams; on the other hand, the innate austerity of natural materials such as marble, stone, exotic woods in gingerbread and earthenware colours, enamelled, tinted or glazed ceramics, used for deep baths, showers and basins, whose soft colours and satin touch symbolize the tones and texture of skin. It is interesting to note that in these intimate surroundings calculated to soothe body and soul, these modern temples of the bath, the accent now is on the element of water itself, and the supreme physical pleasure of water against bare skin.

One of the main trends in decoration is the 'retro' look. Rudolf Nureyev's personal bathroom at his Quai Voltaire home in Paris (facing page) boasted a superb bath in tinned copper. The brass plumbing devised by the antiquarian Serge Volevatch is a faithful reproduction of the Victorian style, but only the tap is old – although it looks as if it would be more suited to a barrel than a bath. Designed by interior decorator Jacques Garcia (above), this contemporary bathroom is decorated in an overblown late nineteenth-century style. The effect is of a theatrical set, with the lavishly appointed bathtub occupying centre stage, advertising the pleasures of bathing in company.

THE SENSUAL DELIGHTS OF THE BATH

TO HAVE a bath in your own home, with hot water whenever you want it, at the temperature you want it, that is the dream-come-true Westerners cherished for centuries. But then, having turned up their noses at showerbaths, dismissed vapour baths, deserted the thermal spas in their droves – and furthermore having imposed their own preferred model on the rest of the world, to the point that other civilizations actually abandoned their inherited traditions – what did they do some twenty years ago? Why, they reappropriated them – hammams, saunas, even thermal spas, those new temples to beauty and fitness, where you surrender yourself to the joys of power-showers, Jacuzzis and all the rest, and rediscover the benefits of the thermal springs and hot water baths in which the Japanese have indulged with a passion since time immemorial.

And now, thanks to modern technology, we can accommodate all these exotic experiences in our own bathrooms – for that, it seems, is the one sensitive point on which our Western culture will never give way.

But have we truly experienced the sensual delights of the bath?

Up to a point, yes. Since the majority has long since been convinced of the virtues of cleanliness, the bath has tended to be seen as combining the beneficial effects of water with the pleasures (or necessity?) of indulging in the cult of the body. For it is the body that has now become the focus of identity, that which expresses the essential truth about an individual. Once it was enough to check one's clothes and make-up in front of a mirror to satisfy the social code. Today it is the whole body that is put on show – and in an increasingly denuded state. As the historian

Georges Duby points out in his *Histoire de la vie privée*: 'being ashamed of your body is more or less the equivalent of being ashamed of yourself.'

Everyone now has to appear younger and more beautiful than ever, fitter, glowing with health, fragrant with cleanliness, with shining hair, impeccably soft skin, and, if possible, a permanent light tan. It is the perfect example of what the historian Norbert Elias in *The Civilizing Process* has called the 'progressive weight of culture on the world of immediate corporeal sensations'.

Yet soaking in the bath is a simple pleasure. And since understanding does not inhibit enjoyment, we should not ignore either the pleasure that comes of knowing we are 'a body immersed in water', obedient to the laws of physics discovered by Archimedes when he took his famous bath and formulated the principle that explains the instant sensation of lightness we experience as we sink into the bath.

You can wile away hours in the tub. Like Ariane in Albert Cohen's *Belle du Seigneur*, who used to spin out the time until her next lovers' tryst. 'At eight in the evening, it was time for the last bath of the day, taken as late as possible so as to be a miracle of impeccability when he arrived.... In the bath she played at poking out her toes and wiggling them, imagining they were her ten children, five little boys on the left, five little girls on the right, ticking them off, telling them to go quickly and have a bath and get to bed, and then she would put them back in the hot water.'

Or you can simply languish there, as Philippe Djian wrote in his novel *Lent dehors*: '... [in this building with its ridiculously severe polished wood and gilding] I am bored most of the time, but in a pleasant kind of way. Rather like being in a foaming bath!'

ALL THESE images invoke the deliciously restorative feeling of water against the skin, in the milky white space of the bathtub. Smiles, sponges and water games sum up four ages of bathing: the 'miraculous comfort' of the photograph of 1930 by Manassé (page 171); the mythologized luxury (facing page) of the Hollywood production, with Gina Lollabrigida's bath in the 1959 extravaganza Solomon and Sheba; *the democratized act (above) in Roy Lichtenstein's canvas of 1963; the refreshment of mind and body, in the image of purity captured in this contemporary photograph by M. Jukkema (page 170).*

IN THE HEAT OF
THE HAMMAM

Tea at a Turkish bath will be mint tea in a little glass. After the steam and the massage, you sit with your companions sipping tea, wrapped in towels, your body wonderfully relaxed and flooded with warmth.

In Arabic, *hamma* means 'to heat'. The idea of hot baths goes back to the days of the Eastern Empire, but the hammam, unlike the original Roman baths, is a place of retreat. Secretive or even poetic in character, it offers spiritual as much as physical purification. In its steamy rooms, the sun does not shine brightly: only a few feeble rays filter though the coloured glass of the honeycomb of little round and star-shaped apertures in the domes. The rays of light hang in the floating steam and lend a sense of enchantment to the murk, whose grey shadows are, it seems, propitious for meeting the djinns that haunt these places. In Russia they are spirits, in Finland they are goblins, for there too the baths are steeped in tradition. The hammam is a magical place, which, according to popular belief, was once thought capable of saving the sick who lay at death's door. Even today the hammam is called the 'silent doctor'.

The Moorish model of the hammam usually takes the form of a suite of marble-clad rooms leading one into another. In the days of the Ottoman Turks, a cross shape was adopted of the type that can still be seen in Istanbul and Cairo. In the centre is the hot room or *beit-al-harara*, which acts as the focal point; fanning off from it like chapels are a number of smaller rooms. In the middle is a raised marble slab called the belly-stone. One would usually lie on this polygonal surface to have a massage. The dry heat is provided by pipes of hot air under the floor. From here you would move on to the steam room, where hot water trickles down from the ceiling and saturates the atmosphere with water vapour. There is a central pool called the *maghtas*.

After the traditional scrubs, massages and stretches comes an all-over wash with soap, followed by a rinse at the fountain, where you use a tinned copper cup to splash yourself with the refreshing cold water. Finally you return to the room where you had left your clothes, the *maslak*, to relax, drink mint tea and enjoy Oriental pastries.

What lingers most in the mind are the sounds. Water splashing against your body or on the floor, rinsing away the dirt as it bubbles down the gutters; the sound of cups clinking, murmured conversations, sometimes the clear tinkle of laughter on women's day; a percussion concert that rings out against the marble and the high ceilings.

Due to its religious origins, the hammam is never mixed. Women's day can always be recognized by the squeals of joy in the entrance hall and the linen hung over the door. It was customary to go there for the whole day, so women would bring baskets of food and clean linen, like the women and girl in Jules Van Biesbroeck's painting *Women Entering a Turkish Bath*.

The narrow definition of the hammam is that it is an extension of the mosque, where the major ablutions are performed in preparation for Friday prayers. But as well as providing for rituals of purification, it became also a place for meditation and retreat, for spiritual exercises performed in a state of heightened sensual awareness, a place therefore for

HAMMAMS ARE places of purification and relaxation, an integral part of the Turkish lifestyle. The Cagaloglu hammam was built in 1741 by Sultan Mahmut I for the city of Istanbul. Then as now, in the darkness of its **hararet** *(steam room) of grey marble, a ray of light falls on the bathers as they wash at the patinated taps of the carved wall-fountains (above), following their steam bath and massage on the heated slab called the 'belly-stone' (facing page). The ritual has scarcely changed since the 18th century, and the account given by Jean de Thévenot in his* **Voyages au Levant**: *'In the big room which is very hot, you sit almost on a level with the floor, which is entirely paved with marble and heated by furnaces beneath. Then a servant comes and makes you lie on your back, puts your knees against your belly and stomach and squeezes you tightly until all the bones in your body, arms and legs crack.'*

both mental and physical relaxation, where nudity blurred all social distinctions.

To gain some idea of the past splendours of the hammams, one needs to visit Istanbul, where several ancient baths have been restored. Admire, for example, the elegance of the marble basins and fountains, the sculpted taps and coloured marble mosaics of the hammam presented to the city in 1741 by Sultan Mahmut I. Its hot room is surmounted by a dome resting on columns; there is another square room covered by a dome flanked with cupolas, and the small side-chambers below are occupied by fountains for ablutions that, the story has it, were built by the famous architect Sinan for the wife of Selim 'the sot'.

Lady Mary Wortley Montagu was already familiar with the atmosphere of the public baths at the time of her visit in 1718 to the private hammam of the Grand Vizier. She recalls her impressions: 'But no part of it pleased me better than the apartments destined for the bagnios. There are two built exactly in the same manner, complementing one another; the baths, fountains and pavements, all of white marble, the roofs gilt, and the walls covered with Japan china; but adjoining them, two rooms, the upper part of which is divided into a sofa; in the four corners water falls from the very roof, from shell to shell, of white marble, to the lower end of the room, where it falls into a large basin, surrounded with pipes, that throw up the water as high as the room. The walls are in the nature of lattices; and, on the outside of them, vines and woodbines planted, that form a sort of green tapestry, and give an agreeable obscurity to these delightful chambers.'

The private hammams in the palaces were fantastic places. In the nineteenth century, the architects tried to outdo one another in the beauty of their marble traceries: sculpted and pierced grey marble in the Ottoman style in the palace of Ciragan (today it forms part of a hotel); Egyptian onyx and Baroque-inspired decoration weighed down with garlands of flowers for the Dolmabahçe. At the Topkapi Palace – which incidentally had over thirty bathrooms – the men's and the women's hammam can still be seen, built of grey-veined white marble and constructed almost like a mirror image on either side of a wall of sculpted marble. The partition is pierced with windows covered over with close-meshed grilles. To retain the heat, the dressing-room was hung with heavily embroidered materials in a myriad of bright colours, and a multitude of cushions would lie scattered on the sofas where people could recline, while the hot room, with its bare marble walls, would be bathed in an opalescent light, the only gleam of colour coming from the gold of the pipes and taps of the fountains.

Although people in these Muslim countries still spend a lot of time in the hammams, as Western-style baths have become more common, so latterly the wealthier classes have deserted them. The hammams have for the most part lost the luxurious appearance described with such enthusiasm by the male and female travellers of the past, and Westerners today are occasionally disappointed by the condition in which they find them. But if you can put that to one side, they remain, as they always were, havens of peace and well-being, and lively and convivial places to visit.

A FAVOURITE place to visit in Istanbul is Küçük Mustafa Pasa, one of the oldest hammams, which has a particularly fine wall-fountain (above). Bath towels in a woman's trousseau used to be elaborately embroidered, particularly those intended for the ritual of the fiancée's bath. Roses were the symbol of the family. Other embroidered motifs were believed to scare away the djinns who lurked in the shadows. They can have had nowhere to hide in the washing room (facing page) of these sumptuous baths with its large glass roof protected by elaborate grilles; this room forms part of the Palace of Dolmabahçe, which was built by the Ottoman sultans in the nineteenth century. The light picks out in gold the subtle designs of interwoven foliage that are carved into the onyx fountains and walls, which inspired Théophile Gautier to write in Constantinople: 'What an intense pleasure it must be, on these tiles as transparent as agates, to abandon your supple members to the clever manipulations of the "tellaks", in a cloud of perfumed steam, under a rain of roses and balsam'.

THE PLEASURES OF THE SCANDINAVIAN SAUNA

Far removed from these Oriental splendours, in the vastness of the far north of Europe there exists another civilization with a passion for bathing and vapour baths. A Finnish proverb says: First build your sauna, then build your house. That just about sums up a country where there is one sauna for every family. Or to put it another way, one for every 3.5 persons, a total of roughly 1.6 million saunas in Finland alone, more than in the rest of the world put together. That suggests the importance accorded to this ancient form of bath that was brought to Fin-

land from Central Asia, via Russia, more than two thousand years ago.

The practice of the vapour bath was closely connected with fire worship, for this is a land where the dark winter months without light would have seemed interminably long. Near the house, a wooden cabin would be built (sometimes set into the ground) and a pit dug in the floor to serve as a hearth. Large pebbles from the river (or better still, volcanic rock) would be heaped on top and heated until they were incandescent. Cold water was then thrown on them to release steam.

Today, some seekers after authenticity reconstruct the old models that are half underground, but most Finns are content to install the traditional

ALTHOUGH THE word 'sauna' is not even one hundred years old, the type of vapour bath that is heated by means of incandescent dry stones in a hearth goes back at least two thousand years. From its origins in Central Asia, it spread slowly into Russia, and from there to northern Europe. Long established in Finland, it has its roots in a rural society where it would have been used by the whole family and farmworkers and servants. In the nineteenth century, under Swedish rule, the intelligentsia claimed the sauna as the symbol of Finnish nationhood. Dating from that period is this 1808 watercolour (above) by C.P. Elfström of a sauna in the region of Oulu in Ostrobothnia. The touching scene shows the timeless gestures (whipping with the vihta to promote sweating in the hottest part of the bath) that are performed for one another, or by one of the bathhouse women. This women's sauna takes place in a large, simple wooden hut, at a time when the vapour room served also as a washing and changing area.

savusauna or smoke sauna, which requires no chimney and is heated by burning wood.

With its roots in the rural societies of Finland and Russia, the sauna is a family bath. Once that term included everyone living under the same roof, even the farmworkers. During the months when the fields were being cultivated, the sauna would be heated up in the evening so the harvesters could soothe their tired and aching muscles in the warmth. The sauna was also used as a grain store; it was here that the malt was dried and meat hung up to smoke. As industrialization got under way in the nineteenth century, the bath became a communal ritual reserved for the end of the working week or the day before a feast day.

Saunas in towns may not enjoy beautiful natural surroundings but otherwise they are built along precisely the same lines. The word 'sauna' actually describes the building itself, which is a small, free-standing cabin of wooden logs. In 1906, the review *Le Magasin pittoresque* contained a description of a 'seano', this being 'a little wooden house near a source of water' consisting of 'a square room with wide benches arranged around the sides; in the centre, the hearth. You heat up the slabs of stone, then throw boiling water on them to create an abundance of steam'. Almost like a doll's house, the sauna usually consists of three rooms: a changing room, which may be furnished; a room for washing, with a bench, a wooden stool and containers of hot and cold water (a shower in town); and, finally, a room for the vapour bath itself. This must be constructed of natural untreated wood, usually fir, but sometimes birch, which releases balsamic essences. The stove is built of brick, or it may take the form of a metal cylinder. The bunks to lie on are made of a lightweight white wood, pine, aspen, poplar or abachi, porous woods that do not get too hot and catch fire. The sauna should be in harmony with nature, situated at the edge of a forest and near a lake, pool or river (not difficult to achieve in Finland).

Of the feminine gender in Finnish, the word 'sauna' represents maternal warmth and security. It was always regarded as a good place, where the significant events of one's life occurred. You were born there, it was the place where you took a symbolic nuptial bath, where you gave birth and where you took sick people on their death bed when they seemed beyond help. Here too the dead were laid out.

It is also an enchanted place, inhabited, it was once thought, by the 'earth spirit' that lurked under the benches. The fairies were supposed to bathe there when the men and women had finished. No one ever knew if it was true because popular superstition forbade you to go and look. Today it is said to be the home of goblins that keep an eye on naughty children.

A place for cleanliness and for recharging the body, it also fulfils a spiritual function for the Finns as a place for relaxation and meditation. A tacit silence is observed, as body and soul unite in the contemplation of a beauty that is internal as much as external. You take your sauna with your family – today in the narrow sense of the word – and at the most a few close friends. It is a great honour to be invited as a guest. It is a sacred place. An old proverb says: In the sauna, behave as if you were in church. Impropriety would be unthinkable, as would noise, raised voices and swearing.

The ritual has scarcely changed at all since the sauna was first invented. As in so many other civilizations, the bath was traditionally taken in the evening, marking the end of the day's work and the retreat into domesticity, or else at the end of the week to prepare for the Lord's Day. Habits nowadays are more fluid, people may have a sauna two or three times a week, or they may have one every day.

THE TRADITIONAL sauna was built away from the house in a small log cabin, sometimes half underground. The earliest saunas were without chimneys and so the room would fill up with smoke from the burning wood used to heat the stones. Before taking your first bath, you would quickly open the door to let it escape. That is what we see happening in the photograph (above) taken in the museum village of Muurame, which features several old saunas dating from before the 1940s. Today the smoke sauna or **savusauna** *has many enthusiasts among the purists. They like to take their first bath in the traditional manner in the 'raw vapour', which becomes impregnated with particles of ash as water is thrown on the stones. The vapour clings to the body and supposedly purifies the skin. And it is true that ash was one of the ingredients of the early soaps, and was used as a washing powder right up to the twentieth century.*

Traditionally you would have entered the sauna dry, although many people today prefer to have a quick wash with soap first in the shower. To get the circulation moving and make the body sweat, you then beat yourself with a small bunch of birch twigs, the *vihta*. This essential accessory to the art of the sauna is cut on Midsummer Day when the leaves and stems are still quite tender. It is salted to keep it green and preserved by hanging it in a cool, well-ventilated spot. If it is well made, it will be an object of beauty that lasts through till the spring of the following year. In the summer, to celebrate the solstice, a bouquet is made up of nine different flowers and trees, among them juniper, alder and birch. After

the bath, one of the bathers stands with his back to the cabin and throws the bouquet over his shoulder and up over the roof. The way the stems are pointing is supposed to indicate the direction from which his or her lover will arrive.

After the first sweat, you go out and splash yourself with water, and then start again. In principle the sauna ends with a *löyly*, which consists in a strong burst of steam intended to intensify the last sweat. Using a ladle with a specially long wooden handle, so you do not burn yourself, you throw onto the hot stones one or two ladlefuls of cold water taken from a little wooden bucket (to which, if desired, a few drops of eucalyptus oil may have been added). The

SAUNAS ARE for good boys and girls, because the goblins who watch over the place know every trick they get up to. These smiling children are sitting in a modern sauna heated by electricity (above).
Today's thinking is that a child of three can start to have regular vapour baths in the company of his parents.
It used to be even younger, and indeed the sauna was once the traditional place for giving birth. Various customs grew up at different times of the year. On Christmas Eve for example, the floor and benches would be symbolically scattered with straw. The whole household would rise early because this was a day that symbolized rebirth, looking forward to the New Year, so that no task must left undone before the hour of the sauna.

water vapour that is given off humidifies the dry air of the sauna, making the room feel even hotter and provoking a particular prickling of the skin that is greatly appreciated by aficionados.

Depending on your inclination and physical condition, you can go on alternating showers and saunas as long as you like. For here as in the hammam or the Japanese *furo*, time disappears in the pleasure of feeling yourself flooded with welcome warmth, in a secure place lit with a dim light that is both peaceful and beautiful. You should hear a Finn talk about the light in the sauna. It needs to be at the lowest level possible, so that you feel at ease with your nakedness. The ideal is the natural light of the country sauna that has no electricity, during the season when it is half-day and half-night, when the building is lit only by two candles between the panes of the double-glazed window or by a single lantern. In winter there may also be a candle in the stove, as far away as possible from the hot stones.

Only when the required feeling of well-being is achieved, does one take the decision to leave. Then it is merely a question of scrubbing the skin in the washing room, with the aid of loofahs or natural brushes (if this is your final exit from the sauna, you will omit the use of soap), and finishing off with a cold shower to allow the body to return to its normal temperature. Purists who live in the country may dive into lakes and sometimes roll in the snow. It is by no means uncommon for people to make a hole in the ice in winter – and not unknown to come very close to being trapped as the ice freezes over.

After a first rub with a natural sponge, you must dry yourself carefully with a rough towel. Since time immemorial, this has been woven from a hemp and flax mixture, but a coarse linen is acceptable. An ordinary towel is much less good, unless it contains a little flax.

Finally, if you wish, you can make your last brief trip into the heat of the sauna, just to warm yourself up. All that then remains is to cover yourself so as not to catch cold and stretch out in comfort, letting your whole body relax, before getting dressed. This is the perfect moment to experience a pleasurable sensation of hunger and thirst. The tradition is to grill so-called sauna sausages over the hearth in the cloakroom and sip a good fresh beer or some *sahti* (a malt drink) with your bathing companions.

The infinite pleasures of heat, water and the natural world, shared with the family in an atmosphere of peace and security – the Finns could not conceive of being without a sauna. You need to share one with them, see the precision of their gestures, watch them make a *vihta*, hear them recount their childhood memories and distant family traditions, if you are even to begin to imagine what these few stones on a hearth mean for them, and the particular poetic associations that accompany the experience. Only then you will understand that we foreign enthusiasts who regularly practice and appreciate the benefits of the sauna can never hope to penetrate the Scandinavian legend.

IN FINLAND, no sauna is without its **vihta** *(above). This is the small bunch of birch twigs used to 'whip up the blood' and make the sweat flow freely. The bundles are assembled in springtime when the stems are still tender, and are hung up for storage in a cool and well-ventilated spot. There is an art to preserving them for as long as possible. If you run out, you have to use winter twigs, which all Finnish children remember for being almost as painful as the strap. Today, thanks to the existence of the freezer, no such problems are likely to arise.*

JAPANESE BATHS: THE ECSTASIES OF THE STEAMING HOT BATH

No other country has quite Japan's passion for baths. As Peter Grilli, author of *Pleasures of the Japanese Bath*, has noted, bathing in Japan is practically a religion. The ethic of bathing is deeply rooted in the Japanese spirit, along with related notions of purity, nature and aesthetics. These have come to dominate all areas of life – art, architecture, literature, crafts, even the presentation and preparation of food, and models of family and social organization. Within that ethical framework the common thread, now and in the past, is the philosophy of Shinto.

In Japan, water is a magical element and a special part of everyday life. Not only is Japan an island, it also possesses more than twenty thousand natural springs, whose waterholes formed the original baths. As long ago as the third century, Chinese travellers noted the habits of cleanliness and rituals of Shinto purification practised by their 'barbarous' neighbours. In the sixth and seventh centuries, with the advent of Confucianism and Buddhism, certain important elements of Chinese culture became influential. Confucianism recommended maintaining and preserving the body, from the smallest patch of skin down to a single hair, because it was inherited from the ancestors, while Buddhism celebrated the virtues of cleanliness in general, and the merit to be gained in future reincarnations from providing baths for the poor and the sick.

For centuries, the Japanese have enjoyed three sorts of baths: the communal public bath called the *sento*, the private bath or *furo* and the *onsen* or natural bath in volcanic springs.

The *sento* was originally a vapour bath, used first in the monasteries and then in the public baths that began to spring up at the start of the seventeenth century. Entering through a sliding door, you would have found yourself in a hot room of sweet-smelling wood, with vats of water bubbling away under the floor. You would have stretched yourself out on a platform and surrendered yourself to the pleasures of the vapour bath and then, having cleansed your skin by scrubbing it with loofahs or little bags of bran, you would have rinsed yourself with hot water in an adjoining room. As everywhere in the world, these public baths were places of licensed conviviality. As a Japanese proverb would have it: Bath friends are best friends. The baths were mixed, which did not seem to set tongues wagging as it did in the West.

There are many descriptions of the *sento* in literature today. In his autobiographical novel *Kôsaku*, the writer Inoue relates: 'Kôsaku also got into the habit when he left school of going to the public bath in the valley.... He began to go down there almost every day. For Kôsaku, bathing meant being able to enjoy a moment of peace.... He liked to walk on his own for a bit first, without having to bother about anyone else, and then sit on the edge of the bath in the afternoon, when there was absolutely no one there.'

We can also gain some idea of the ancient *sento* from films of traditional Japan, such as those

IN JAPAN, the presence of public baths is often signalled by this logo (facing page, bottom).
The photograph of the familiar ritual of the daily bath (facing page, top) was not taken by a Japanese but by one of the first great documenters of the Eastern world, the Venetian Felice Beato. He went to Japan in 1863 for a fortnight's visit, and used the time to capture the traditional Japanese life of the period in a series of evocative compositions. The Japanese girls are the focus of the picture, but it is important to note the wooden vat with its iron hoops, connected by a pipe to a small brazier for heating water. In the early twentieth century, the wooden vessel was replaced by one made of iron, so that the water could be heated directly from below. A perfect replica of these ancient wooden bath vats is to be seen in the Zen-inspired bathroom of the American-Japanese sculptor Nogushi, who regularly retreats to his house on the island of Shikoku, in the south of the Japanese archipelago (above).

directed by Mizoguchi. There is the familiar clack of wooden clogs in the street on the way to the baths, the sound of the soap being batted about as the bathers paddle on the bottoms of their small wooden tubs – these they always brought with them, wrapped in the traditional *furoshiki*, a square of cloth used as a carrying bag. At the beginning of the seventeenth century, the cloth was also used as a mat to recline on after the bath and, so that people could recognize their own, they dyed them in different colours or marked them with their family crests. Finally, there would be the colourful spectacle of entire families walking slowly home for supper, their skins reddened, their bodies rested and swathed in the traditional *yukata* of cotton muslin.

For a large number of Japanese, these enduring memories are more than simple nostalgia for the past. Even the majority who have their own bathrooms are conscious that they are missing out on what is perhaps the essential, the company of other people, and so they return from time to time to the *sento*. It is a way of keeping up a sense of community, reinforcing old ties, making new friends and – since they are distinguished by nothing but their nakedness – of encouraging the different social classes to interact, by exchanging views or swapping local gossip. It is also an opportunity for relaxation and reflection in neutral surroundings, where a person can be alone even while surrounded by other people. There is an expression in Japanese, *hadaka no tsukiai*, which means literally 'companions in nudity'; it is used to describe closest friends as well as casual companions met at the baths. After the bath, you stay on for a beer and some sushi and

you are bound to carry on talking or join in a game of *go*. The atmosphere has not really changed very much since the old days.

The private bath, or *furo*, has a ritual of its own, although the elements are just the same: a water tap, a little footstool, a bucket, a deep bath. The contemporary urban home may have dispensed with the traditional, smooth-surfaced vat of fragrant wood, and the little garden outside, but it is still to the *furo* that the Japanese will turn to satisfy a passion for bathing that is without a doubt the most cerebral and the most consuming in the world.

Even to begin to appreciate what a Japanese person feels about his bath, you have to pay close attention not only to his words, but also to his silences and the expression on his face. Just the thought of the *furo* makes him imagine he is there. A happy smile plays over his lips, his eyes go misty, and if you look deep into them you see him sitting up to his chin in hot water, the steaming hot clear water of the deep bath that is the *furo*. The heat steals over him and impregnates his whole body, while his spirit escapes and gently floats away. And if as a good European you ask him how long he stays in the bath, he will reply that it depends, that once the tensions have evaporated, sometimes your sense of well-being and harmony with nature will be such that you may start chanting *haikus*, or even composing your own.

You yourself may not be much further forward (except that you feel faintly jealous), but at least you have understood one thing, that the Japanese daily bath is not really about cleanliness as such, but about spiritual cleanliness. For if you want to be

THE JAPANESE bath called the furo *is long enough for the bather to lie flat and has a lid to keep the water hot. Cypress wood is the material favoured for the modern* furo *(above). In a traditional dwelling, the bathroom was situated in a separate small building of its own, with a tiny garden adjacent; the interior was entirely of wood, as were the bath itself and all the accessories, a stool and a bowl for washing the body before immersion. The intrusion of modern comfort has made very little difference to the traditional order. The pleasures of the private bath notwithstanding, the Japanese still like to go into town to visit the* sento, *or to the hot springs to benefit from the* onsen, *where they enjoy communal baths with their* hadaka no tsukiai *or 'companions in nudity'. The Hoshi Onsen of Gummaken (facing page) is equipped with a superb traditional wooden building.*

clean, it is not necessary to bathe every day. This is something that transcends physical hygiene. The bath cleanses the spirit and restores it to a state of peace, almost of innocence, so laying up a 'stock' of generosity and tolerance for the future. Significantly, there used to be a ritual according to which, at times of social unrest or before important sea voyages, you would elect someone to go without baths, so that he would become the scapegoat for the community's future ills. If the worst outcome was averted, he was allowed to bathe again. If not, he was put to death.

For centuries, the Japanese bath has provided daily refreshment for the spirit, and warmth and cleanliness for the body. The ancient practice of bathing before dinner has continued up to the present day. In principle it is the father who opens the ceremony, followed by the mother and children, who all bathe in the same water – which never gets dirty because everyone has already washed beforehand and is therefore impeccably clean from the start.

The traditional bath is easily large enough to accommodate two people sitting. The oldest type is a rectangular wooden structure 172 centimetres (66 inches) long, 84 centimetres (33 inches) wide and 56 centimetres (22 inches) deep. It may be made of any one of a number of sweet-smelling woods such as Japanese cypress, cryptomeria, chestnut or Chinese black pine. Today it would cost a fortune to buy a traditional bath of this kind, which has to be made of wood that has been aged. The modern bath is shorter and wider, but the depth is unchanged, being calculated to enable a person to sit in the water up to the chin, and in a sufficient volume of water to be slightly afloat, while not actually rising to the surface.

The essence of the Japanese bath is to slip into very hot water and then stay there and enjoy it as long as the mood takes you. After this indeterminate period of basking in the warmth and euphoria, you emerge and slip on a marvellous dressing-gown called a *yukata*. Once this garment was worn for taking the few steps separating the *furo* from the dining room, for in the traditional home the *furo* was in a small building set apart from the house, ensuring that the bath was as quiet and undisturbed as possible. The structure was made entirely of wood and gave onto the indispensable small garden that symbolized the natural world. Laid out with great care, although not necessarily according to Zen principles, the garden was positioned so that it could be viewed from the bathtub. Today such installations are only to be found in the countryside and in de luxe apartments, where people are still concerned with preserving the aesthetic traditions of the culture of their ancestors. For a traditional *furo* does not consist only of the bathtub itself: it is an entire space that must be constructed according to very precise specifications, from the materials used for the floor and the walls, to the lighting (diffuse) and the heating of the room (underfloor) and, most particularly, of the water.

However, any Japanese person will tell you that the crowning experience of the bath is the ecstasy of contemplating the garden, whose carefully chosen elements are the indispensable means of pacifying the body and letting the spirit roam free, after the torpor and gentle euphoria induced by the hot water. To discover today's equivalent of this ordered calm, one has to stay in a *ryokan*, one of those country inns built near the hot springs or *onsen*. There you can enjoy the rare pleasure of bathing in nature; there the lifestyle of ancestral Japan persists.

The Japanese have enthused about their open-air

PURITY, NATURE and beauty: these three concepts are fundamental to the Japanese ethic, and to the practice of bathing in particular. They are experienced at their height in the onsen *(thermal spas), which exist in their thousands in Japan. To the north of Tokyo, the hot springs of Takagarawa (facing page, top and bottom) provide an opportunity to bathe naked, as there are separate baths for men and women. The spa is situated in exceptionally beautiful countryside, with waterfalls and natural ponds, and swimming pools sheltering under roofs of a traditional design. There in the steamy air you can abandon yourself to reverie or meditation, as in this photograph by Françoise Lemarchand (above) taken at the baths of the* ryokan *(traditional inn) at the Kanaya springs, near the town of Kanasawa. Not all the* onsen *are as poetic. Many are modern complexes visited by coachloads of Japanese at the weekend. But the enthusiasm for the practice indicates the extent of their passion for bathing.*

baths for more than two thousand years, and doubtless the roots of their passion lie deeper still in their history. To float happily in hot water in fabulous natural surroundings, in summer to the accompaniment of a symphony of birdsong, rustling leaves and hissing waterfalls, in winter in the muffled silence of sparkling snow, to allow the current of waterfalls to play endlessly over the length of their bodies – that is an experience that induces in them an inexpressible euphoria and a deep sense of being at one with the elements.

All the greatest twentieth-century Japanese writers have included bathing scenes in their novels. The incomparable Yasunari Kawabata has celebrated them in works such as *Snowy Land* and *The Dancer of Izu*, both set in thermal spas. In *Maidservants of the Inns*, he takes nature and water as his principal characters. 'O-Taki raised O-Yuki in his arms like an armful of green vegetables and sprang from stone to stone.... The moon's reflections shimmered all around like a multitude of migratory birds plunging into the deep water. The whiteness of the rocks enclosed their absolute nakedness.... You heard the thud of the small wooden buckets the others were putting down on the cement tiles after they finished cleaning the baths.... The room that held the baths was a sort of glasshouse with a stone-paved floor. A large basin was divided into three areas. In the first, hot water flowed in torrents, spilling over into the second, and so on once again, in such a way that it became cooler as it went.'

THE NATURAL BATHROOM: BATHING AS LIFESTYLE

Since the 1950s, the Japanese have adopted many elements of our lifestyle, but their bathing practices have remained virtually unchanged, while we in the West, on the contrary, have been inspired to try to adapt something of their Shinto spirit to our cold and impersonal bathrooms.

The 'natural' bathroom is part of this movement, the result of a worldwide reappraisal of the dwelling-house that has its roots in the work of Rudolf Steiner and Frank Lloyd Wright. The former was a German anthropologist at the turn of the century who explored traditional habitats; the second was the celebrated American architect who was the pioneer during the 1930s of houses that 'merged' with the natural world. Wright made particular use of running water in cascades and basins as an element of exterior decoration, drawing on these symbols of fertility, life and purity to create harmonious and satisfying environments. In 1989 the well-known architect and ecologist David Pearson wrote *The Natural House Book*, a bestselling publication on contemporary American architecture. Developing the fundamental concept of the bathroom as an extension of the natural world, he proceeded to integrate that idea with the broad principles of modern ecology, taking the private baths and outdoor communal baths of the Japanese as the basis for his reflections on the joys of water.

IN THE tree-covered mountains above the Black Sea in Turkey, between the humid mists from the sky and the waters of the river Firtina, live the Hemsinli people. They have preserved to this day their traditional way of life, and their magnificent dwellings with imposing blue and white wooden façades perched on high stone foundations. Each family member has his or her own room, which serves as living room, bedroom and bathroom. A large bucket of water heated in the kitchen, a pot of cold water and a cake of soap (above): those are all you need to take your place in the bathtub concealed beneath wooden boards and surrender yourself to the pleasures of hot water. The same simplicity and charm characterize this famous shot by Willy Ronis (facing page). His Provençal Nude *of 1949 is both graceful and poetic, and its elemental gestures of washing face and hands seem to encapsulate all other such gestures that have gone before. The bowl on its elegant iron stand has the sort of simplicity that inspired Philippe Starck's design for a washbasin that is, in essence, a basin standing on a table.*

As the bathroom is a place for physical and mental renewal, the atmosphere should, above all, make you want to spend time there. You are absolutely naked, and therefore defenceless, so you must feel safe in the room. It should be as comfortable as possible, and dedicated to well-being, repose and contemplation. The ambient colours and lighting should be soothing. Being in an osmotic relationship with nature, the bathroom should be extended by means of a large window or door opening onto a garden containing running water, so that there is a gentle splashing sound accompanying your bath, or in town by a little internal conservatory to provide the necessary link with nature. The room should be hot (25° C or 77° F) and kept ventilated constantly.

The technical equipment should be carefully chosen with maximum comfort and safety in mind.

Underfloor heating is recommended, because you will walk about barefoot. That is also why tiled floors and rugs need to be non-slip. The low-level light sources should be concealed behind screens controlled by cords; there should be no switches or points, except one with alternating current for an electric razor, next to the basin. Behind the appliances, the walls should be tiled – everywhere else they should be of natural microporous materials that breathe – plaster, certain special paints, cork or untreated wood: the ideal, as in Japan, being cypress or cedar that give off subtle scents when exposed to humidity.

The bath should be large, if it is to be shared by the whole family. For the greatest satisfaction, it should be as deep as possible (set partly into a raised platform) so that you can enjoy that slight sensation of

THE 'NATURAL' bathroom (above) belongs to the house at Punta del Este owned by the painter Uriburu. It corresponds to the architect David Pearson's belief that the bathroom should be stimulating, relaxing and restorative, but above all a place where you want to spend time. This sort of 'ecological' design has its roots in the work of Frank Lloyd Wright and the ideas of Rudolf Steiner, as well as in Japanese domestic architecture. Uriburu was famous in the age of the 'happening' for painting the Grand Canal in Venice green, but here he has chosen blue for the surround of his sunken bath, which is set into a bay window that overlooks the beach. The bather is in close intimacy with nature and can linger in the soft water as he lets his thoughts roam free over the wide open spaces of the ocean.

weightlessness, as in Japan, and keep your shoulders completely submerged. A small heating element to keep the water at a constant temperature would be the perfect solution, but you can also adopt the medieval expedient of hanging a curtain round the bath to retain the heat and trap the steam. A heated towel rail is a must, for warm towels when you emerge.

The shower is absolutely essential, so that you can wash before entering the bath. And to adapt the room for small children, the author recommends installing a large shower base of sufficient depth for them to use as a mini-bath. Finally, a space should be created for exercise, and there should be a chair to relax in or a bench that can be used for massage, to complete the pleasures of the bath. To make the atmosphere as intimate and welcoming as possible, you can add a few items of furniture, not forgetting a low footstool on which to sit finally and relax in the bath, as the Japanese do, or to sit on while in the shower so that you can wash the children, for example, without straining your back. The bathroom can be extended into the garden by installing its counterpart outside in the open air. It would include a big spa or hot tub for the pleasure of bathing with friends under the trees.

A PRISTINE vegetable sponge, soaps made with natural ingredients or producing a soft, milky foam,
a sachet to soften the water and imbue it with delicious fragrances, a few candles and music to suit your mood,
that more or less is the definition of a bath made in heaven. Candles and music apart, the products that bear
the brandname 'Côte bastide' (above) offer you all this and more. Until the invention of the vegetable sponge
in the 1930s, only those natural sponges qualified as 'medicinal' found their way to the bathroom.
They are fished for in the sea off Tunisia, Greece and Turkey, and since the 1920s have also been cultivated.
The invention of true soap has been dated by historians to around AD 1302, when animal fats were replaced by
vegetable fats. Cakes of toilet soap, however, are a relatively recent invention and first appeared in about 1579. It
was in the reign of Louis XIV that the standards for the manufacture of 'Marseille soap' were laid down;
it was meant to contain a minimum of 72 per cent olive oil, while cream soaps could be made of copra,
groundnut, rapeseed or palm oil.

THE VIRTUES OF THERMAL SPAS AND BALNEOTHERAPY

Today many of the traditional delights of bathing seem to be subsumed in the newly rediscovered practice of hydrotherapy. The move began with thalassotherapy – the use of sea water cures – which was developed in France by Louison Bobet, and which subsequently provoked a resurgence of interest in the benefits of thermal spas. The ancient enthusiasm for these watering places has its modern counterpart in health farms visited by the wealthy, where they pursue a fitness regime that includes balneotherapy. In France, Evian, Vittel, Aix-les-Bains, Vichy, Luchon, Molitg-les-Bains and Eugénie-les-Bains are among the best-known centres. The last in particular prides itself on the splendid establishment run by Christine and Michel Guérard, whose Ferme d'Eugénie would no doubt have delighted the Empress who led the fashion for the waters of the town in the nineteenth century.

This exceptional place more or less sums up the pleasures of balneotherapy. You can enjoy the delicious natural foods of the so-called 'active' *cuisine minceur*, while you indulge in a variety of ultrasophisticated treatments including various types of bath – Druidic with medicinal herbs, Roman with fragrant oils or Turkish with its distinctive aromas and purifying steam. An essential component of all the baths and showers, whether water massages, power jets or plant infusions, is the heavily mineralized water from the hot spring that has flowed in the countryside outside Eugénie for thousands of years.

There too you may enjoy baths with the most inspirational ingredients – like the 'Queen's floral' relaxation bath: an infusion of spa water with red rosebuds, lavender, camomile and hawthorn, with a little bag of these same flowers to inhale and pat on the body. Or the 'weightless' bath with kaolin, a bath of fine white mud enriched with thermal plankton, in which, as you slowly immerse yourself in its creamy consistency, your body feels weightless, dissolving away all the tensions and making the skin feel incredibly soft.

Back in favour too are baths perfumed with the aromatic plants and essential oils whose beneficial effects have been known since prehistoric times. And there are countless other baths and treatments to make the skin soft, among them famous recipes left for posterity by great figures from the past – like the bath of crushed pearls favoured by Cleopatra, Poppea's bath of asses' milk, the baths of raspberries, pineapple and strawberries devised by Madame Tallien, even the cow's milk baths of Cardinal Richelieu (a man, at last), which his servants used to sell when he had finished!

HUNGARY, LIKE JAPAN, abounds in hot springs. The most famous baths in Budapest are at the Gellert Hotel, built in 1918 in a Neo-classical and late Art Nouveau style; there is a whiff of Mitteleuropa here that is endlessly fascinating to the traveller. It is essential to visit the superb turquoise mosaic hot baths for men (pages 194–95) and the swimming pool, covered by a glass roof and flanked (facing page) by a mezzanine with balconies supported on cable columns. An ultrasophisticated ambience is combined with the traditional hospitality of the Landes at the Eugénie-les-Bains health farm (above) where, along with the delights and benefits of the spring water favoured by the Empress, you can also enjoy Michel Guérard's secret recipe for a unique purifying bath that is made from a mixture of spring water and kaolin, the opalescent powder used for Limoges porcelain. The result is a cream bath of incomparable softness in which you float weightlessly, within a clover-shaped bath designed by Christine Guérard. Absolute bliss.

193

Are these merely the caprices of the famous or do they actually work? Either way, the efficacy of the bran and almond bath is beyond dispute. It has been known for centuries, and there are several different recipes. At the end of the nineteenth century, it used to be made with four ounces of sweet almonds, a pound of sweet pine nuts, a pound of inula root, ten handfuls of linseed, a handful of marshmallow root and a few lily bulbs, all pounded up together. The resulting paste was then put into a sachet and plunged in the bath. Some beauty treatments were made from preparations that were bizarre to say the least, among them such concoctions as baths of cinnabar, wine lees, tripe and meat broth, and a mixture made of milk and the broth of white chicken meat and calves' feet!

Others were extraordinary not so much because of their ingredients as because of the elaborate or unusual lengths to which people went in order to increase the sensual pleasure of the experience. Paul Cuisin describes at the end of his guide the 'Portuguese women's bath', which was taken in the evening with candles burning and Aeolian harps suspended at the windows so that the wind would make the strings vibrate 'producing ravishing sounds'. He also describes the bath of Madame de Barançay, 'the most original thing in the world'. Just before the close of day, she would immerse herself in her bath, which was 'lit with candles, and hung between two garlands of artificial roses, and swung imperceptibly with the aid of a mechanical pendulum'.

To reproduce the illusion of that delicious feeling of running water against the body, that inimitable soft caress of the waves or the current, when in fact you are lying immobile in a bath, is an ancient fantasy that has teased people's imaginations over the centuries and produced some quite astonishing solutions. One was the German 'rocking' bath, a sort of canoe-shaped vessel on a rocker, in which the bather moved the water to and fro by pulling hard on the front with both arms.

The dream was finally realized by Roy Jacuzzi. It is his name that has become the generic name for this type of massage bath. Jacuzzi was descended from an Italian family who emigrated to California at the beginning of the twentieth century, settled in Berkeley and founded a factory for the manufacture of aircraft fans (later of aircraft). He invented the first 'whirlpool' bath in 1966, which he called the Roman bath. The bathwater is sucked up by a hydraulic pump into a pipe, along which it is propelled at speed; it is then augmented by an inflow of air, which increases its force as it passes back into the bathtub, through holes called 'buses'. The positioning of these holes in the bathtub is calculated in relation to the situation of the bather's body and the precise angle of the jets. The bubbles created by the mixture of water and air provide a micromassage that is reviving, relaxing and toning. In tune with the mood of the 1970s, Jacuzzi went on to invent the Adonis, a bath for two, then the Oversize for multiple occupation. Today, the company has some two hundred and fifty patents, including one that reproduces the famous Japanese massage called *shiatsu*, using 32 underwater jets that correspond to the principal meridians running through the body. The system took four years to develop. The water pressure is controlled by a computer and creates a continuous rolling motion, rather like that produced by the fingers in shiatsu massage. Upwardly directed jets from below are followed by downwardly directed jets from above, which have a toning and relaxing effect. Today all the major brandnames have their own range of

IN THE nineteenth century, the thermal spas benefited from sumptuous architectural settings that are reminiscent as much of cathedrals as of the splendours of the baths of antiquity. Synonymous with social elitism, places for pampering and for leisure pursuits, at different periods one might have encountered at the Thermes Nationaux d'Aix-les-Bains, or at least at the tables of the nearby casino, Queen Victoria, Eva Perón, Stanley Baldwin, Rose Fouilloux, King Baudouin of Belgium or the Aga Khan, whose favourite bathtub is illustrated (above). Encased in small squares of cast glass, it incorporates a mural representing a spray of water with tiny champagne-like bubbles. Baden-Baden is probably the most famous of the spa towns and today, buffeted by winds and spray, it retains the atmosphere of the luxurious and romantic encounters of a bygone age. The 'Emperor Frederick's Baths' (facing page) are in a state of perfect preservation; they occupy the site of the Roman baths built by Caracalla in the third century AD.

massage baths, which work on the same principle of compressed water and air. As these are propelled at speed into the bath, the air provides the relaxing massage and the water the toning massage. The jets may be of varying intensity. Some models also use ozone, which opens the pores and deep-cleans and softens the skin. These appliances all use the latest technology and have very strict safety standards. All models are provided with a waterproof remote control that can be used to adjust the settings, programme the length of the massage and even switch on music. Recently a Belgian manufacturer offered a model with baffles incorporated in the sides, which could transmit sound underwater when you were completely submerged. Last but not least is the built-in spotlight that illuminates the water, making these hot tubs more and more like swimming pools. There are models to accommodate three to seven people. They are never emptied: the water is simply heated, filtered and recycled, exactly like a swimming pool. Often known as 'spas', they are sold increasingly to private individuals at the very top end of the market, especially in the United States and in Germany, where they are installed on the veranda, in the fitness area or in the garden. But they are most often found in hotels, fitness centres and gym clubs.

With the growing number of enthusiasts for these bracing water massages has come the invention of showers with specially adapted power jets; judiciously positioned, the 'buses' can provide massages for the back, legs, calves and even the soles of the feet. The system can be added on to a traditional shower, but the future lies in the fully-fitted cabins that are already on sale, many of which also contain the equipment for a steam bath. These cabins can be easily connected to the existing plumbing and have proved a huge success in the United States, especially with a younger clientele who do not own their homes: when you move, you simply take your power shower with you.

But the very finest bath experience technology has to offer must be the installation made by the sanitary ware manufacturer Kohler. This American giant is a family-based enterprise, as big as the town from which it takes its name. When it was set up at the end of the nineteenth century, it was no more than a small foundry that had perfected the process of enamelling a cast-iron horse-trough. According to the company's advertising, someone looked at this trough one day and thought if it was stood on four feet it would make a fine bathtub.

Kohler's latest innovation is an extraordinary 'cell', practically a small room. The interior is lined with teak, it has a sliding glass door and a removable cypress-wood floor, or a mattress of upholstered waterproof material, that conceals a large massage bath with head-cushions. The cabin is large enough for two, and all its functions are programmable – sauna, hammam, a simulation of the heat of the sun or the caress of a summer breeze, and a cool shower that descends from the ceiling like a spring dew. In its sealed environment that subsumes within it all of nature and the bathing practices of the entire world, one can almost imagine living contentedly in a state of virtual self-sufficiency within its comforting womb-like interior.

It is an idea that had occurred to the hero of Philippe Toussaint's novel *La Salle de bains*, even though he had nothing like that sophisticated technology: 'When I began to spend my afternoons in the bathroom, I had no intention of moving in; I just used to spend some agreeable hours there, meditating in the bath, occasionally fully clothed, sometimes naked.... I would accompany my words with expansive gestures, and I thought that the most practical bathtubs were those with parallel sides, with a sloping back, and an upright end which saved the occupant from having to use the foot-rest.... [Then when I ended up living there entirely] I used to lie in the bath all afternoon and meditate peacefully with my eyes shut, with that feeling of extraordinary pertinence you get from thoughts that there is no need to put into words.'

THE POETRY OF THE BATH

As our exploration of the art of bathing, over the centuries and through various civilizations, draws to an end, we find that we have come almost full circle, so closely does our modern practice of daily ablutions resemble the original purposes of purity and renewal. For our rituals touch on some of the most ancient and obvious symbolic associations of water. And thanks to the miracles of technology, the bathroom of today incorporates them all. In immersion, there is a re-turn to the origins of life, to the womb. In splashing on of water, the restoration of purity. In balneotherapy, the power of water to renew and heal.

Not only does our bathwater clean the dirt from our body, it also dissolves our mental tensions. 'I was trembling with cold and felt only a deep need to soak in very hot water, in a rather acid aromatic bath, a bath like those in which you take refuge in Paris on cold winter mornings,' wrote Colette in *La Naissance du Jour*, after parting from a loved one. It is an idea explored in Peter Greenaway's metaphorical film *The Pillow Book*, where the heroine escapes her past by painting onto naked bodies Japanese ideograms taken from a diary, which then disperse in water.

At the end of the twentieth century, splashing water over ourselves or immersing ourselves in water echoes the symbolic function of the Fountain of Eternal Youth, that famous natural spring so often depicted in pre-Renaissance paintings.

A fountain basin or a bathtub, good pure water, a pool below a waterfall or a spring; these sum up the quintessential pleasures of the bath, as personified by Victor Ségalen in *Stèles*: 'My lover has the virtues of water: a clear smile, flowing gestures, a pure voice that echoes pearlingly.'

'The purity and freshness of water combine to provide that special sense of joy with which all lovers of water are familiar, [in which] the union of the sensible and the sensual takes on a higher significance,' wrote Gaston Bachelard, concluding: 'so hygiene – or as we would say today, the bath – becomes a "poem".'

In this book, the works of painters, engravers, photographers and writers have provided poetry aplenty. Let Anatole France supply the last words with a few lines from his poem *Le Bain*: 'La baignoire s'emplit sous deux filets limpides./ Dans la salle où l'odeur des bois vient par moments,/ L'enfant, qu'apprête encor la mère aux doigts rapides,/ Rit de voir tour à tour tomber ses vêtements./ Voici la noble éponge et les brosses acerbes,/ Le savon onctueux, les sels en blancs cristeaux,/ La peigne aux longues dents, la toile aux parfums d'herbes,/ Les poissons aimantés, le cygne et les bateaux..../ Ainsi la mère invite, et persuade et presse,/ Et plonge enfin le corps frêle et nerveux,/ Et lui, que réjouit la fluide caresse,/ S'agite et rit de voir dégoutter ses cheveux.' (The bath fills up from two limpid streams/ In the room where the smell of the woods comes and goes/ The child, still made ready by the mother's agile fingers/ Laughs to see its clothes fall off in turn/ Here are the noble sponge and the harsh brushes/ The greasy soap, the white crystal salts/ The long-toothed comb, the herb-scented cloth/ The magnetic fish, the swan and boats. .../ The mother invites, cajoles, insists/ And plunges in at last the frail and nervous body/ And he, cheered by the liquid caress/ Wriggles and laughs as he shakes water from his hair.)

Whatever the threats to 'the purity and freshness of water', for our own delight let us hope that we will be able to preserve for ever the poetry of the bath.

To SHOWER or bathe in the open air is a pleasure that architects and interior decorators have tried to recreate in recent installations of bathrooms in hotels and summer houses. The pioneers in this were undoubtedly the English, experts at 'camping out' in Africa, where they would arrive with their luggage full of English comforts: folding bathtubs, rubber tubs and portable showers. We are at the dawn of an age in which the water supply is beset with problems and uncertainties, where we cannot ignore pollution and the waste of resources. Perhaps this African shower (above) points the way ahead? The traditional Finnish sauna ends in an invigorating rub with coarse towels made of the traditional flax, like this exquisite two-toned bath linen by Johanna Gullichsen (page 200), in a robust craft-weave that becomes more beautiful every time it is washed.

CHRONOLOGY

BIBLIOGRAPHY

PHOTO CREDITS

INDEX

ACKNOWLEDGMENTS

CHRONOLOGY

Antiquity

An oblong earthenware bath – the ancestor of the modern bath – was installed in the palace of King Minos at Knossos in Crete c. 1800 BC.

Oblong and oval marble baths first used in the first century BC in the Roman *thermae*.

Middle Ages

Bathing takes place in the public bath-houses or in private, in round or oval iron-hooped wooden bath vats, placed in bedrooms.

First reference in 1292 to delivery of bathing water to households by water carriers in Paris, a practice continued until 1890.

Fourteenth century

First use of metal baths.

Improvements made to methods of heating water, with the wooden bath vat being fed by a pipe connected to a cauldron of hot water on a small stove; metal baths were also placed directly above a heat source.

Seventeenth century

In the luxurious *appartements de bains* of the French aristocracy, marble bathtubs were supplied with water from tanks on the floor above, filled by servants and placed over a wood-burning fire.

Eighteenth century

Metal bathtubs now in general use; they were normally made of tinned copper because it does not rust and retains heat well.

First bathtubs disguised as wickerwork or upholstered sofas, couches or chaises-longues, produced by cabinetmakers.

First 'boot' or slipper bath of a type similar to that used by Marat and Benjamin Franklin.

Vogue for footbaths, arm-baths, sitz-baths, etc., for part-body washing.

The elegant console washstand of the Renaissance period replaced by a small, finely made cabinet with drawers and fitted compartments.

First mention of the bidet in literature, used at this time by both men and women.

Inexpensive iron baths, with a painted enamel surface, appeared c. 1770.

Public baths installed in riverboats in the capital cities of Western Europe at the end of the century.

1800 to 1850

Expansion of the service supplying baths to homes.

Zinc baths appeared.

In addition to the riverboats, new public baths opened in Western European cities in areas recently connected to the water supply.

The simple washstand with basin and ewer superseded by a substantial chest-of-drawers with overmantel, inset porcelain basin and built-in water tank: an English invention.

c. 1850

The gas-fuelled water-heater, an English invention, introduced.

c. 1870

The English bathroom reaches its peak of popularity: it has running water from the mains, washbasin, large porcelain bathtubs and gas water-heater with thermostat.

Vogue for the tub, a type of sponge bath of English origin that uses less water than a full bath.

c. 1880

Increasing numbers of households in Western cities connected to the water supply. Introduction of the first water meters in Paris.

The cast-iron bathtub, an English invention, appeared.

1900s

Process of covering cast-iron baths with enamel, using a spray technique, perfected; the bath sheet is thus rendered obsolete.

The large, cast-iron bathtub with curved rim and lion's-paw feet introduced.

First porcelain pedestal washbasins.

First wall-mounted water-heaters (Porcher).

First free-standing showers.

1920s

Mass production of the moulded, one-piece, enamelled cast-iron bath.

1950s

The hand shower with hose enters general use.

1960s

Invention of the whirlpool bath by the American designer Roy Jacuzzi.

Leading designers involved in bathroom design from the late 1960s.

1970s

First mixer taps (Ideal Standard).

1980s

With the introduction of acrylics in every shade and colour, basins and baths now made in a variety of forms, e.g., corner baths and double 'shells' combining bath and shower. Large manufacturers of sanitary ware sign up leading designers for their top-of-the range lines.

1990s

Invention of the thermostatically controlled mixer tap.

Leading manufacturers of bathroom appliances move increasingly towards products that save water and energy.

Development of facilities for balneotherapy in the home.

BIBLIOGRAPHY

Allen, E.: *Wash and Brush Up.* London, 1976.

Ashe, G.: *The Tale of the Tub.* London, 1950.

Bachelard, Gaston: *L'Eau et les rêves.* Paris, 1945.

Balsdon, J. P. V. D.: *Life and Leisure in Ancient Rome.* New York, 1969.

Barrett, Helena, and Phillips, John: *Suburban Style: The British Home, 1840–1960.* London, 1987.

Beard, Geoffrey: *The National Trust Book of the English House Interior.* London, 1991.

Cabanes, Dr: *Moeurs intimes du passé: La vie aux bains.* Paris, 1909.

Clark, Scott: *Japan: A View from the Bath.* Honolulu, 1994.

Conran, Terence: *The Bed and Bath Book.* London, 1978.

Cuisin, Paul: *Les Bains de Paris et des principales villes du monde.* Paris, 1822.

Cunliffe, Barry W.: *Roman Bath Discovered.* London, 1984.

Dunant, David: *Life in the Country House: A Historical Dictionary.* London, 1996.

Eassie, W.: *Sanitary Arrangements for Dwellings.* London, 1874.

Eleb, M., and Debarre-Blanchard, A.: *Architectures de la vie privée: Maison et mentalités, XVII–XIXe siècles.* Brussels, 1989.

Elias, Norbert: *The Civilizing Process.* Oxford and Cambridge, MA, 1994.

Forty, Adrian: *Objects of Desire: Design and Society since 1750.* London, 1986.

Franklin, Alfred: *La vie privée d'autrefois: Arts et métiers, modes, moeurs, usages des Parisiens du XIIe au XVIIIe siècle.* Paris, 1888.

Garches, Marquise de: *Les Secrets de beauté d'une Parisienne.* Paris, 1894.

Garrett, Elisabeth Donaghy: *At Home: The American Family, 1750–1870.* New York, 1990.

Gencé, Comtesse de: *Le Cabinet de toilette d'une honnête femme.* Paris, 1909.

Giedion, Siegfried: *Mechanization Takes Command.* New York, 1948.

Girouard, Mark: *Life in the English Country House: A Social and Architectural History.* New Haven, 1978.

Girouard, Mark: *The Victorian Country House.* New Haven, 1979.

Greuter, Lise: *Villes d'eaux en France.* Paris, 1985.

Hellyer, S. Stevens: *The Plumber and Sanitary Houses.* London, 1877.

Hellyer, S. Stevens: *The Principles and Practices of Plumbing.* London, 1891.

Hicks, David: *David Hicks on Bathrooms.* Oxford, 1970.

Kira, Alexander: *The Bathroom.* New York and Harmondsworth, 1976.

Koren, Leonard: *Undesigning the Bath.* Berkeley, CA, 1996.

Lambton, Lucinda: *Temples of Convenience and Chambers of Delight.* London, 1995.

Laty, Dominique: *Histoire des bains.*

Leistner, Dieter: *The Water Temple.* London, 1994.

Long, Helen C.: *The Edwardian House: The Middle-Class Home in Britain, 1880–1914.* Manchester, 1993.

Lupton, Ellen, and Miller, J. Abbott: *The Bathroom, the Kitchen and the Aesthetics of Waste: A Process of Elimination.* Cambridge, MA, 1992.

Manser, Jose: *Bathrooms.* London, 1969.

Négrier, Paul: *Les Bains à travers les âges.* Paris, 1925.

Palmer, Roy: *The Water Closet: A New History.* Newton Abbot, 1973.

Perrot, Philippe: *Le Luxe: Une richesse entre faste et confort.* Paris, 1995.

Reyburn, Wallace: *Flushed with Pride: The Story of Thomas Crapper.* London, 1969, reprinted 1989.

Reynolds, Reginald: *Cleanliness and Godliness.* London, 1943.

Robins, F. W.: *The Story of Water Supply.* Oxford, 1946.

Rudolfsky, Bernard: 'Uncleanliness and Ungodliness: A Rapid Survey of Bathing Costumes and Bathroom History', *Interior Design*, June 1984, pp. 212–21.

Scott, G. B.: *The Story of Baths and Bathing.* London, 1939.

Staffe, Baronne de: *Le Cabinet de toilette.* Paris, 1903.

Thornton, Peter: *Authentic Decor: The Domestic Interior, 1620–1920.* London, 1984.

Vigarello, Georges: *Le Propre et le Sale.* Paris, 1985.

Winkler, Gail Caskey: *The Well-appointed Bath: Authentic Plans and Fixtures from the Early 1900s.* Washington, DC, 1989.

Wright, Lawrence: *Clean and Decent: The Fascinating History of the Bathroom and the Water Closet.* London, 1960.

Yeghul, Fikret K.: *Baths and Bathing in Classical Antiquity.* New York and Cambridge, MA, 1992.

PHOTO CREDITS

INDEX

ACKNOWLEDGMENTS

The author wishes to thank Nathalie Bailleux, Marc Walter and Maryse Hubert for their invaluable assistance, and also Anne-Laure Mojaïsky, Soazig Cudennec, Aurélie Prissette and Lydie Sébire.

She owes a particular debt of gratitude to Annie Lecat and to everyone else who placed their knowledge at her disposal in the course of her research, either indirectly – through works referred to by name in this volume (Norbert Elias, Philippe Perrot, Anne de Marnhac, Georges Vigarello, Jean-Pierre Goubert, Peter Grilli and Lawrence Wright) and to José Alvarez for the remarkable documentation contained in his monographs and other writings on design and the decorative arts – or directly, by providing information that has contributed to the text (Jean-François Baillet, Nicolas Béboutoff, Lena Brossard, Michèle Congé, Shelley Cossonnet, Victoire Gaignault, Anne-Marie Goussard, Elisabeth Loeb, Yasuko Pinard, Massimo Berti, Jean-Paul Deschamps,

Jussi Kosonen, Jacques Henocq, Naokasu Masuda, Michel Perret-Ducray, Stéphane Sibony, Cyrille Schmeller and Serge Volevatch).

She owes a great debt of gratitude to everyone who allowed her access to places of particular interest (Isabelle Juppé, Agnès Leboeuf, Claude Hombert, Nicole Pluvieux, Madame Winklarick, Thierry Balesdent, Yves Carlier and Bernard Collette) or to particular documents (Annette Nebut) and would like to acknowledge the kindness of Paule-Andrée Moselle and Brigitte Gaumerais in placing permanently at her disposal all the catalogues and back issues of magazines in the collections of the Bibliothèque Forney. Finally, she would like to thank Dr Jean-Pierre Duboc, President of the Association Française du Sauna, and everyone who responded to her enquiries for factual information.

The publishers would particularly like to thank Madame Johanna Gullichsen, who very kindly lent all the sauna accessories, Madame Sirkku Dölle of the National

Museum of Finland for her ready assistance in sending the illustrations required, Madame Christine Guérard for her welcoming response to our enquiries, Madame Sterling from the Galerie Lestranger at Saint-Rémy-de-Provence, Monsieur Kramer for the welcome we received in Schiltach and for the documentation provided, and Monsieur Gabriel Detourne.

Particular thanks are due to Messieurs Richard and Philippe Grohe of the Hansgrohe firm, whose enthusiasm for the art of bathing matched that of the team involved in this project, and to Leonard Koren, whose book *Undesigning the Bath* contributed so greatly to our understanding of the subject.

Finally, thanks are due to the team without whose work this book would not have been possible: Nathalie Bailleux, Margherita Mariano, Murielle Vaux, Anne-Laure Mojaïsky, Véronique Manssy, Soazig Cudennec, Cécile Guillaume, Carine Lefeuvre and Aurélie Prissette.